D1323724

1 3 5 7 9 10 8 6 4 2

Vintage
20 Vauxhall Bridge Road,
London SW1V 2SA

Vintage Classics is part of the Penguin Random House
group of companies whose addresses can be found at
global.penguinrandomhouse.com

Penguin
Random House
UK

Sapiens was first published in Great Britain by Harvill Secker in 2014
Homo Deus was first published in Great Britain by Harvill Secker in 2016
This edition published by Vintage in 2018

penguin.co.uk/vintage

A CIP catalogue record for this book is available from the British Library

ISBN 9781784874025

Typeset in 9.5/14.5 pt FreightText Pro
by Jouve (UK), Milton Keynes
Printed and bound by Clays Ltd, St Ives plc

Penguin Random House is committed to a sustainable future for
our business, our readers and our planet. This book is made from
Forest Stewardship Council® certified paper.

Money

YUVAL NOAH HARARI

VINTAGE MINIS

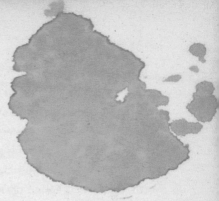

The Scent of Money

In 1519 Hernán Cortés and his Conquistadors invaded Mexico, hitherto an isolated human world. The Aztecs, as the people who lived there called themselves, quickly noticed that the aliens showed an extraordinary interest in a certain yellow metal. In fact, they never seemed to stop talking about it. The natives were not unfamiliar with gold – it was pretty and easy to work, so they used it to make jewellery and statues, and they occasionally used gold dust as a medium of exchange. But when an Aztec wanted to buy something, he generally paid in cocoa beans or bolts of cloth. The Spanish obsession with gold thus seemed inexplicable. What was so important about a metal that could not be eaten, drunk or woven, and was too soft to use for tools or weapons? When the natives questioned Cortés as to why the Spaniards had such a passion for gold, the conquistador answered, 'Because I and my companions suffer from a disease of the heart which can be cured only with gold.'

In the Afro-Asian world from which the Spaniards came, the obsession for gold was indeed an epidemic. Even the bitterest of enemies lusted after the same useless yellow metal. Three centuries before the conquest of Mexico, the ancestors of Cortés and his army waged a bloody war of religion against the Muslim kingdoms in Iberia and North Africa. The followers of Christ and the followers of Allah killed each other by the thousands, devastated fields and orchards, and turned prosperous cities into smouldering ruins – all for the greater glory of Christ or Allah.

As the Christians gradually gained the upper hand, they marked their victories not only by destroying mosques and building churches, but also by issuing new gold and silver coins bearing the sign of the cross and thanking God for His help in combating the infidels. Yet alongside the new currency, the victors minted another type of coin, called the millares, which carried a somewhat different message. These square coins made by the Christian conquerors were emblazoned with flowing Arabic script that declared: 'There is no god except Allah, and Muhammad is Allah's messenger.' Even the Catholic bishops of Melgueil and Agde issued these faithful copies of popular Muslim coins, and God-fearing Christians happily used them.

Tolerance flourished on the other side of the hill too. Muslim merchants in North Africa conducted business using Christian coins such as the Florentine florin, the Venetian ducat and the Neapolitan gigliato. Even Muslim rulers who called for jihad against the infidel Christians were glad to receive taxes in coins that invoked Christ and His Virgin Mother.

How Much Is It?

HUNTER-GATHERERS HAD no money. Each band hunted, gathered and manufactured almost everything it required, from meat to medicine, from sandals to sorcery. Different band members may have specialised in different tasks, but they shared their goods and services through an economy of favours and obligations. A piece of meat given for free would carry with it the assumption of reciprocity – say, free medical assistance. The band was economically independent; only a few rare items that could not be found locally – seashells, pigments, obsidian and the like – had to be obtained from strangers. This could usually be done by simple barter: 'We'll give you pretty seashells, and you'll give us high-quality flint.'

Little of this changed with the onset of the Agricultural Revolution. Most people continued to live in small, intimate communities. Much like a hunter-gatherer band, each village was a self-sufficient economic unit, maintained by mutual favours and obligations plus a little barter with outsiders. One villager may have been particularly adept at making shoes, another at dispensing medical care, so villagers knew where to turn when barefoot or sick. But villages were small and their economies limited, so there could be no full-time shoemakers and doctors.

The rise of cities and kingdoms and the improvement in transport infrastructure brought about new opportunities for specialisation. Densely populated cities provided full-time employment not just for professional shoemakers and doctors, but also for carpenters, priests, soldiers and lawyers. Villages that gained a reputation for producing really good wine, olive oil or ceramics discovered that it was worth their while to specialise nearly exclusively in that product and trade it with other settlements for all the other goods they needed. This made a lot of sense. Climates and soils differ, so why drink mediocre wine from your backyard if you can buy a smoother variety from a place whose soil and climate is much better suited to grape vines? If the clay in your backyard makes stronger and prettier pots, then you can make an exchange. Furthermore, full-time specialist vintners and potters, not to mention doctors and lawyers, can hone their expertise to the benefit of all. But specialisation created a problem – how do you manage the exchange of goods between the specialists?

An economy of favours and obligations doesn't work when large numbers of strangers try to cooperate. It's one thing to provide free assistance to a sister or a neighbour, a very different thing to take care of foreigners who might never reciprocate the favour. One can fall back on barter. But barter is effective only when exchanging a limited range of products. It cannot form the basis for a complex economy.

In order to understand the limitations of barter, imagine that you own an apple orchard in the hill country that produces the crispest, sweetest apples in the entire province. You work so hard in your orchard that your shoes wear out. So you harness up your donkey cart and head to the market town down by the river. Your neighbour told you that a shoemaker on the south end of the marketplace made him a really sturdy pair of boots that's lasted him through five seasons. You find the shoemaker's shop and offer to barter some of your apples in exchange for the shoes you need.

The shoemaker hesitates. How many apples should he ask for in payment? Every day he encounters dozens of customers, a few of whom bring along sacks of apples, while others carry wheat, goats or cloth – all of varying quality. Still others offer their expertise in petitioning the king or curing backaches. The last time the shoemaker exchanged shoes for apples was three months ago, and back then he asked for three sacks of apples. Or was it four? But come to think of it, those apples were sour valley apples, rather than prime hill apples. On the other hand, on that previous occasion, the apples were given in exchange for small women's shoes. This fellow is asking for man-size boots. Besides, in recent weeks a disease has decimated the flocks around town, and skins are becoming scarce. The tanners are starting to demand twice as many finished shoes in exchange for the same quantity of leather. Shouldn't that be taken into consideration?

In a barter economy, every day the shoemaker and the apple grower will have to learn anew the relative prices of dozens of commodities. If one hundred different commodities are traded in the market, then buyers and sellers will have to know 4,950 different exchange rates. And if 1,000 different commodities are traded, buyers and sellers must juggle 499,500 different exchange rates! How do you figure it out?

It gets worse. Even if you manage to calculate how many apples equal one pair of shoes, barter is not always possible. After all, a trade requires that each side want what the other has to offer. What happens if the shoemaker doesn't like apples and if, at the moment in question, what he really wants is a divorce? True, the farmer could look for a lawyer who likes apples and set up a three-way deal. But what if the lawyer is full up on apples but really needs a haircut?

Some societies tried to solve the problem by establishing a central barter system that collected products from specialist growers and manufacturers and distributed them to those who needed them. The largest and most famous such experiment was conducted in the Soviet Union, and it failed miserably. 'Everyone would work according to their abilities, and receive according to their needs' turned out in practice into 'everyone would work as little as they can get away with, and receive as much as they could grab'. More moderate and more successful experiments were made on other occasions, for example in the Inca Empire. Yet most societies found a more easy way to connect large numbers of experts – they developed money.

Shells and Cigarettes

MONEY WAS CREATED many times in many places. Its development required no technological breakthroughs – it was a purely mental revolution. It involved the creation of a new inter-subjective reality that exists solely in people's shared imagination.

Money is not coins and banknotes. Money is anything that people are willing to use in order to represent systematically the value of other things for the purpose of exchanging goods and services. Money enables people to compare quickly and easily the value of different commodities (such as apples, shoes and divorces), to easily exchange one thing for another, and to store wealth conveniently. There have been many types of money. The most familiar is the coin, which is a standardised piece of imprinted metal. Yet money existed long before the invention of coinage, and cultures have prospered using other things as currency, such as shells, cattle, skins, salt, grain, beads, cloth and promissory notes. Cowry shells were used as money for about 4,000 years all over Africa, South Asia, East Asia and Oceania. Taxes could still be paid in cowry shells in British Uganda in the early twentieth century.

In modern prisons and POW camps, cigarettes have

often served as money. Even non-smoking prisoners have been willing to accept cigarettes in payment, and to calculate the value of all other goods and services in cigarettes. One Auschwitz survivor described the cigarette currency used in the camp: 'We had our own currency, whose value no one questioned: the cigarette. The price of every article was stated in cigarettes ... In "normal" times, that is, when the candidates to the gas chambers were coming in at a regular pace, a loaf of bread cost twelve cigarettes; a 300-gram package of margarine, thirty; a watch, eighty to 200; a litre of alcohol, 400 cigarettes!'

In fact, even today coins and banknotes are a rare form of money. The sum total of money in the world is about $60 trillion, yet the sum total of coins and banknotes is less than $6 trillion. More than 90 per cent of all money – more than $50 trillion appearing in our accounts – exists only on computer servers. Accordingly, most business transactions are executed by moving electronic data from one computer file to another, without any exchange of physical cash. Only a criminal buys a house, for example, by handing over a suitcase full of banknotes. As long as people are willing to trade goods and services in exchange for electronic data, it's even better than shiny coins and crisp banknotes – lighter, less bulky, and easier to keep track of.

For complex commercial systems to function, some kind of money is indispensable. A shoemaker in a money economy needs to know only the prices charged for various kinds of shoes – there is no need to memorise the exchange rates between shoes and apples or goats. Money also frees apple experts from the need to search out apple-craving shoemakers, because everyone always wants money. This is perhaps its most basic quality. Everyone always wants money because everyone else also always wants money, which means you can exchange money for whatever you want or need. The shoemaker will always be happy to take your money, because no matter what he really wants – apples, goats or a divorce – he can get it in exchange for money.

Money is thus a universal medium of exchange that enables people to convert almost everything into almost anything else. Brawn gets converted to brain when a dis-charged soldier finances his college tuition with his military benefits. Land gets converted into loyalty when a baron sells property to support his retainers. Health is converted to justice when a physician uses her fees to hire a lawyer – or bribe a judge. It is even possible to convert sex into salvation, as fifteenth-century prostitutes did when they slept with men for money, which they in turn used to buy indulgences from the Catholic Church.

Ideal types of money enable people not merely to turn one thing into another, but to store wealth as well. Many valuables cannot be stored – such as time or beauty. Some things can be stored only for a short time, such as straw-berries. Other things are more durable, but take up a lot of space and require expensive facilities and care. Grain, for example, can be stored for years, but to do so you need to build huge storehouses and guard against rats, mould, water, fire and thieves. Money, whether paper, computer bits or cowry shells, solves these problems. Cowry shells don't rot, are unpalatable to rats, can survive fires and are compact enough to be locked up in a safe.

In order to use wealth it is not enough just to store it. It often needs to be transported from place to place. Some forms of wealth, such as real estate, cannot be transported at all. Commodities such as wheat and rice can be transported only with difficulty. Imagine a wealthy farmer living in a moneyless land who emigrates to a distant province. His wealth consists mainly of his house and rice paddies. The farmer cannot take with him the house or the paddies. He might exchange them for tons of rice, but it would be very burdensome and expensive to transport all that rice. Money solves these problems. The farmer can sell his property in exchange for a sack of cowry shells, which he can easily carry wherever he goes.

Because money can convert, store and transport wealth easily and cheaply, it made a vital contribution to the appearance of complex commercial networks and dynamic markets. Without money, commercial networks and markets would have been doomed to remain very limited in their size, complexity and dynamism.

How Does Money Work?

COWRY SHELLS AND dollars have value only in our common imagination. Their worth is not inherent in the chemical structure of the shells and paper, or their colour, or their shape. In other words, money isn't a material reality – it is a psychological construct. It works by converting matter into mind. But why does it succeed? Why should anyone be willing to exchange a fertile rice paddy for a handful of useless cowry shells? Why are you willing to flip hamburgers, sell health insurance or babysit three obnoxious brats when all you get for your exertions is a few pieces of coloured paper?

People are willing to do such things when they trust the figments of their collective imagination. Trust is the raw material from which all types of money are minted. When a wealthy farmer sold his possessions for a sack of cowry shells and travelled with them to another province, he trusted that upon reaching his destination other people would be willing to sell him rice, houses and fields in exchange for the shells. Money is accordingly a system of mutual trust, and not just any system of mutual trust: *money is the most universal and most efficient system of mutual trust ever devised.*

What created this trust was a very complex and long-term network of political, social and economic relations. Why do I believe in the cowry shell or gold coin or dollar bill? Because my neighbours believe in them. And my

Why are you willing to flip hamburgers, sell health insurance or babysit three obnoxious brats when all you get for your exertions is a few pieces of coloured paper?

neighbours believe in them because I believe in them. And we all believe in them because our king believes in them and demands them in taxes, and because our priest believes in them and demands them in tithes. Take a dollar bill and look at it carefully. You will see that it is simply a colourful piece of paper with the signature of the US secretary of the treasury on one side, and the slogan 'In God we trust' on the other. We accept the dollar in payment, because we trust in God and the US secretary of the treasury. The crucial role of trust explains why our financial systems are so tightly bound up with our political, social and ideological systems, why financial crises are often triggered by political developments, and why the stock market can rise or fall depending on the way traders feel on a particular morning.

Initially, when the first versions of money were created, people didn't have this sort of trust, so it was necessary to define as 'money' things that had real intrinsic value. History's first known money – Sumerian barley money – is a good example. It appeared in Sumer around 3000 BC, at the same time and place, and under the same circumstances, in which writing appeared. Just as writing developed to answer the needs of intensifying administrative activities, so barley money developed to answer the needs of intensifying economic activities.

Barley money was simply barley – fixed amounts of barley grains used as a universal measure for evaluating and exchanging all other goods and services. The most common measurement was the sila, equivalent to roughly one litre. Standardised bowls, each capable of containing one sila, were mass-produced so that whenever people needed to buy or sell anything, it was easy to measure the necessary amounts of barley. Salaries, too, were set and paid in silas of barley. A male labourer earned sixty silas a month, a female labourer thirty silas. A foreman could earn between 1,200 and 5,000 silas. Not even the most ravenous foreman could eat 5,000 litres of barley a month, but he could use the silas he didn't eat to buy all sorts of other commodities – oil, goats, slaves, and something else to eat besides barley.

Even though barley has intrinsic value, it was not easy to convince people to use it as *money* rather than as just another commodity. In order to understand why, just think what would happen if you took a sack full of barley to your local shopping centre, and tried to buy a shirt or a pizza. The vendors would probably call security. Still, it was somewhat easier to build trust in barley as the first type of money, because barley has an inherent biological value. Humans can eat it. On the other hand, it was difficult to store and transport barley. The real breakthrough in monetary history occurred when people gained trust in money that lacked inherent value, but was easier to store and transport. Such money appeared in ancient Mesopotamia in the middle of the third millennium BC. This was the silver shekel.

The silver shekel was not a coin, but rather 8.33 grams of silver. When Hammurabi's Code declared that a superior man who killed a slave woman must pay her owner twenty silver shekels, it meant that he had to pay 166 grams of silver, not twenty coins. Most monetary terms in the Old Testament are given in terms of silver rather than coins. Joseph's brothers sold him to the Ishmaelites for twenty silver shekels, or rather 166 grams of silver (the same price as a slave woman – he was a youth, after all).

Unlike the barley sila, the silver shekel had no inherent value. You cannot eat, drink or clothe yourself in silver, and it's too soft for making useful tools – ploughshares or swords of silver would crumple almost as fast as ones made out of aluminium foil. When they are used for anything, silver and gold are made into jewellery, crowns and other status symbols – luxury goods that members of a particular culture identify with high social status. Their value is purely cultural.

SET WEIGHTS OF precious metals eventually gave birth to coins. The first coins in history were struck around 640 BC by King Alyattes of Lydia, in western Anatolia. These coins had a standardised weight of gold or silver, and were imprinted with an identification mark. The mark testified to two things. First, it indicated how much precious metal the coin contained. Second, it identified the authority that issued the coin and that guaranteed its contents. Almost all coins in use today are descendants of the Lydian coins.

Coins had two important advantages over unmarked metal ingots. First, the latter had to be weighed for every transaction. Second, weighing the ingot is not enough. How does the shoemaker know that the silver ingot I put down for my boots is really made of pure silver, and not of lead covered on the outside by a thin silver coating? Coins help solve these problems. The mark imprinted on them testifies to their exact value, so the shoemaker doesn't have to keep a scale on his cash register. More importantly, the mark on the coin is the signature of some political authority that guarantees the coin's value.

The shape and size of the mark varied tremendously throughout history, but the message was always the same: 'I, the Great King So-And-So, give you my personal word that this metal disc contains exactly five grams of gold. If anyone dares counterfeit this coin, it means he is fabricating my own signature, which would be a blot on my reputation. I will punish such a crime with the utmost severity.' That's why counterfeiting money has always been considered a much more serious crime than other acts of deception. Counterfeiting is not just cheating – it's a breach of sovereignty, an act of subversion against the power, privileges and person of the king. The legal term is lese-majesty (violating majesty), and was typically punished by torture and death. As long as people trusted the power and integrity of the king, they trusted his coins. Total strangers could easily agree on the worth of a Roman denarius coin, because they trusted the power and integrity of the Roman emperor, whose name and picture adorned it.

In turn, the power of the emperor rested on the denarius. Just think how difficult it would have been to maintain the Roman Empire without coins – if the emperor had to raise taxes and pay salaries in barley and wheat. It would have been impossible to collect barley taxes in Syria, transport the funds to the central treasury in Rome, and transport them again to Britain in order to pay the legions there. It would have been equally difficult to maintain the empire if the inhabitants of the city of Rome believed in gold coins, but the subject populations rejected this belief, putting their trust instead in cowry shells, ivory beads or rolls of cloth.

The Gospel of Gold

THE TRUST IN Rome's coins was so strong that even outside the empire's borders, people were happy to receive payment in denarii. In the first century AD, Roman coins were an accepted medium of exchange in the markets of India, even though the closest Roman legion was thousands of kilometres away. The Indians had such a strong confidence in the denarius and the image of the emperor that when local rulers struck coins of their own they closely imitated the denarius, down to the portrait of the Roman emperor! The name 'denarius' became a generic name for coins. Muslim caliphs Arabicised this name and issued 'dinars'. The dinar is still the official name of the currency in Jordan, Iraq, Serbia, Macedonia, Tunisia and several other countries.

As Lydian-style coinage was spreading from the Mediterranean to the Indian Ocean, China developed a slightly different monetary system, based on bronze coins and unmarked silver and gold ingots. Yet the two monetary systems had enough in common (especially the reliance on gold and silver) that close monetary and commercial relations were established between the Chinese zone and the Lydian zone. Muslim and European merchants and conquerors gradually spread the Lydian system and the gospel of gold to the far corners of the earth. By the late modern era the entire world was a single monetary zone, relying first on gold and silver, and later on a few trusted currencies such as the British pound and the American dollar.

The appearance of a single transnational and transcultural monetary zone laid the foundation for the unification of Afro-Asia, and eventually of the entire globe, into a single economic and political sphere. People continued to speak mutually incomprehensible languages, obey different rulers and worship distinct gods, but all believed in gold and silver and in gold and silver coins. Without this shared belief, global trading networks would have been virtually impossible. The gold and silver that sixteenth-century conquistadors found in America enabled European merchants to buy silk, porcelain and spices in East Asia, thereby moving the wheels of economic growth in both Europe and East Asia. Most of the gold and silver mined in Mexico and the Andes slipped through European fingers to find a welcome home in the purses of Chinese silk and porcelain manufacturers. What would have happened to the global economy if the Chinese hadn't suffered from the same 'disease of the heart' that afflicted Cortés and his companions – and had refused to accept payment in gold and silver?

Yet why should Chinese, Indians, Muslims and Spaniards – who belonged to very different cultures that failed to agree about much of anything – nevertheless share the belief in gold? Why didn't it happen that Spaniards believed in gold, while Muslims believed in barley, Indians in cowry shells, and Chinese in rolls of silk? Economists have a ready answer. Once trade connects two areas, the forces of supply and demand tend to equalise the prices of transportable goods. In order to understand why, consider a hypothetical case. Assume that when regular trade opened between India and the Mediterranean, Indians were uninterested in gold, so it was almost worthless. But in the Mediterranean, gold was a coveted status symbol, hence its value was high. What would happen next?

Merchants travelling between India and the Mediterranean would notice the difference in the value of gold. In order to make a profit, they would buy gold cheaply in India and sell it dearly in the Mediterranean. Consequently, the demand for gold in India would skyrocket, as would its value. At the same time the Mediterranean would experience an influx of gold, whose value would consequently drop. Within a short time the value of gold in India and the Mediterranean would be quite similar. The mere fact that Mediterranean people believed in gold would cause Indians to start believing in it as well. Even if Indians still had no real use for gold, the fact that Mediterranean people wanted it would be enough to make the Indians value it.

Similarly, the fact that another person believes in cowry shells, or dollars, or electronic data, is enough to strengthen our own belief in them, even if that person is otherwise hated, despised or ridiculed by us. Christians and Muslims who could not agree on religious beliefs could nevertheless agree on a monetary belief, because whereas religion asks us to believe in something, money asks us to believe that *other people believe in something*.

For thousand of years, philosophers, thinkers and prophets have besmirched money and called it the root of all evil. Be that as it may, money is also the apogee of human tolerance. Money is more open-minded than language, state laws, cultural codes, religious beliefs and social habits. Money is the only trust system created by humans that can bridge almost any cultural gap, and that does not discriminate on the basis of religion, gender, race, age or sexual orientation. Thanks to money, even people who don't know each other and don't trust each other can nevertheless cooperate effectively.

The Price of Money

MONEY IS BASED on two universal principles:

a. Universal convertibility: with money as an alchemist, you can turn land into loyalty, justice into health, and violence into knowledge.
b. Universal trust: with money as a go-between, any two people can cooperate on any project.

These principles have enabled millions of strangers to cooperate effectively in trade and industry. But these seemingly benign principles have a dark side. When everything is convertible, and when trust depends on anonymous coins and cowry shells, it corrodes local traditions, intimate relations and human values, replacing them with the cold laws of supply and demand.

Human communities and families have always been based on belief in 'priceless' things, such as honour, loyalty, morality and love. These things lie outside the domain of the market, and they shouldn't be bought or sold for money. Even if the market offers a good price, certain things just aren't done. Parents mustn't sell their children into slavery; a devout Christian must not commit a mortal sin; a loyal knight must never betray his lord; and ancestral tribal lands should never be sold to foreigners.

Money has always tried to break through these

barriers, like water seeping through cracks in a dam. Parents have been reduced to selling some of their children into slavery in order to buy food for the others. Devout Christians have murdered, stolen and cheated – and later used their spoils to buy forgiveness from the Church. Ambitious knights auctioned their allegiance to the highest bidder, while securing the loyalty of their own followers by cash payments. Tribal lands were sold to foreigners from the other side of the world in order to purchase an entry ticket into the global economy.

Money has an even darker side. For although money builds universal trust between strangers, this trust is invested not in humans, communities or sacred values, but in money itself and in the impersonal systems that back it. We do not trust the stranger, or the next-door neighbour – we trust the coin they hold. If they run out of coins, we run out of trust. As money brings down the dams of community, religion and state, the world is in danger of becoming one big and rather heartless marketplace.

Hence the economic history of humankind is a delicate dance. People rely on money to facilitate cooperation with strangers, but they're afraid it will corrupt human values and intimate relations. With one hand people willingly destroy the communal dams that held at bay the movement of money and commerce for so long. Yet with the other hand they build new dams to protect society, religion and the environment from enslavement to market forces.

The Capitalist Creed

MONEY HAS BEEN essential both for building empires and for promoting science. But is money the ultimate goal of these undertakings, or perhaps just a dangerous necessity?

It is not easy to grasp the true role of economics in modern history. Whole volumes have been written about how money founded states and ruined them, opened new horizons and enslaved millions, moved the wheels of industry and drove hundreds of species into extinction. Yet to understand modern economic history, you really need to understand just a single word. The word is growth. For better or worse, in sickness and in health, the modern economy has been growing like a hormone-soused teenager. It eats up everything it can find and puts on inches faster than you can count.

For most of history the economy stayed much the same size. Yes, global production increased, but this was due mostly to demographic expansion and the settlement of new lands. Per capita production remained static. But all that changed in the modern age. In 1500, global production of goods and services was equal to about $250 billion; today it hovers around $60 trillion. More importantly, in 1500, annual per capita production averaged $550, while today every man, woman and child produces, on the average, $8,800 a year. What accounts for this stupendous growth?

Economics is a notoriously complicated subject. To make things easier, let's imagine a simple example.

Samuel Greedy, a shrewd financier, founds a bank in El Dorado, California.

A. A. Stone, an up-and-coming contractor in El Dorado, finishes his first big job, receiving payment in cash to the tune of $1 million. He deposits this sum in Mr Greedy's bank. The bank now has $1 million in capital.

In the meantime, Jane McDoughnut, an experienced but impecunious El Dorado chef, thinks she sees a business opportunity – there's no really good bakery in her part of town. But she doesn't have enough money of her own to buy a proper facility complete with industrial ovens, sinks, knives and pots. She goes to the bank, presents her business plan to Greedy, and persuades him that it's a worthwhile investment. He issues her a $1 million loan, by crediting her account in the bank with that sum.

McDoughnut now hires Stone, the contractor, to build and furnish her bakery. His price is $1,000,000.

When she pays him, with a cheque drawn on her

account, Stone deposits it in his account in the Greedy bank.

So how much money does Stone have in his bank account? Right, $2 million.

How much money – cash – is actually located in the bank's safe? Yes, $1 million.

It doesn't stop there. As contractors are wont to do, two months into the job Stone informs McDoughnut that, due to unforeseen problems and expenses, the bill for constructing the bakery will actually be $2 million. Mrs McDoughnut is not pleased, but she can hardly stop the job in the middle. So she pays another visit to the bank, convinces Mr Greedy to give her an additional loan, and he puts another $1 million in her account. She transfers the money to the contractor's account.

How much money does Stone have in his account now? He's got $3 million.

But how much money is actually sitting in the bank? Still just $1 million. In fact, the same $1 million that's been in the bank all along.

Current US banking law permits the bank to repeat this exercise seven more times. The contractor would eventually have $10 million in his account, even though the bank still has but $1 million in its vaults. Banks are allowed to loan $10 for every dollar they actually possess, which means that 90 per cent of all the money in our bank accounts is not covered by actual coins and notes. If all of the account holders at Barclays Bank suddenly demand their money, Barclays will promptly collapse (unless the government steps in to save it). The same is true of Lloyds, Deutsche Bank, Citibank, and all other banks in the world.

It sounds like a giant Ponzi scheme, doesn't it? But if it's a fraud, then the entire modern economy is a fraud. The fact is, it's not a deception, but rather a tribute to the amazing abilities of the human imagination. What enables banks – and the entire economy – to survive and flourish is our trust in the future. This trust is the sole backing for most of the money in the world.

In the bakery example, the discrepancy between the contractor's account statement and the amount of money actually in the bank is Mrs McDoughnut's bakery. Mr Greedy has put the bank's money into the asset, trusting that one day it would be profitable. The bakery hasn't baked a loaf of bread yet, but McDoughnut and Greedy anticipate that a year hence it will be selling thousands of loaves, rolls, cakes and cookies each day, at a handsome profit. Mrs McDoughnut will then be able to repay her loan, with interest. If at that point Mr Stone decides to withdraw his savings, Greedy will be able to come up with the cash. The entire enterprise is thus founded on trust in an imaginary future – the trust that the entrepreneur and the banker have in the bakery of their dreams, along with the contractor's trust in the future solvency of the bank.

We've already seen that money is an astounding thing because it can represent myriad different objects and convert anything into almost anything else. However, before the modern era this ability was limited. In most cases, money could represent and convert only things that actually existed in the present. This imposed a severe limitation on growth, since it made it very hard to finance new enterprises.

Consider our bakery again. Could McDoughnut get it built if money could represent only tangible objects? No. In the present, she has a lot of dreams, but no tangible resources. The only way she could get her bakery built would be to find a contractor willing to work today and receive payment in a few years' time, if and when the bakery starts making money. Alas, such contractors are rare breeds. So our entrepreneur is in a bind. Without a bakery, she can't bake cakes. Without cakes, she can't make money. Without money, she can't hire a contractor. Without a contractor, she has no bakery.

Humankind was trapped in this predicament for thousands of years. As a result, economies remained frozen. The way out of the trap was discovered only in the modern era, with the appearance of a new system based on trust in the future. In it, people agreed to represent imaginary goods – goods that do not exist in the present – with a special kind of money they called 'credit'. Credit enables us to build the present at the expense of the future. It's founded on the assumption that our future resources are sure to be far more abundant than our present resources. A host of new and wonderful opportunities open up if we can build things in the present using future income.

IF CREDIT IS such a wonderful thing, why did nobody think of it earlier? Of course they did. Credit arrangements of one kind or another have existed in all known human cultures, going back at least to ancient Sumer. The problem in previous eras was not that no one had the idea or knew how to use it. It was that people seldom wanted to extend much credit because they didn't trust that the future would be better than the present. They generally believed that times past had been better than their own times and that the future would be worse, or at best much the same. To put that in economic terms, they believed that the total amount of wealth was limited, if not dwindling. People therefore considered it a bad bet to assume that they personally, or their kingdom, or the entire world, would be producing more wealth ten years down the line. Business looked like a zero-sum game. Of course, the profits of one particular bakery might rise, but only at the expense of the bakery next door. Venice might flourish, but only by impoverishing Genoa. The king of England might enrich himself, but only by robbing the king of France. You could cut the pie in many different ways, but it never got any bigger.

That's why many cultures concluded that making bundles of money was sinful. As Jesus said, 'It is easier for a camel to pass through the eye of a needle than for a rich man to enter into the kingdom of God' (Matthew 19:24). If the pie is static, and I have a big part of it, then I must have taken somebody else's slice. The rich were obliged to do penance for their evil deeds by giving some of their surplus wealth to charity.

If the global pie stayed the same size, there was no margin for credit. Credit is the difference between today's pie and tomorrow's pie. If the pie stays the same, why extend credit? It would be an unacceptable risk unless you believed that the baker or king asking for your money might be able to steal a slice from a competitor. So it was hard to get a loan in the premodern world, and when you got one it was usually *small, short-term, and subject to high interest rates*. Upstart entrepreneurs thus found it difficult to open new bakeries and great kings who wanted to build palaces or wage wars had no choice but to raise the necessary funds through high taxes and tariffs. That was fine for kings (as long as their subjects remained docile), but a scullery maid who had a great idea for a bakery and wanted to move up in the world generally could only dream of wealth while scrubbing down the royal kitchen's floors.

It was lose-lose. Because credit was limited, people had trouble financing new businesses. Because there were few new businesses, the economy did not grow. Because it did not grow, people assumed it never would, and those who had capital were wary of extending credit. The expectation of stagnation fulfilled itself.

A Growing Pie

THEN CAME THE Scientific Revolution and the idea of progress. The idea of progress is built on the notion that if we admit our ignorance and invest resources in research, things can improve. This idea was soon translated into economic terms. Whoever believes in progress believes that geographical discoveries, technological inventions and organisational developments can increase the sum total of human production, trade and wealth. New trade routes in the Atlantic could flourish without ruining old routes in the Indian Ocean. New goods could be produced without reducing the production of old ones. For instance, one could open a new bakery specialising in chocolate cakes and croissants without causing bakeries specialising in bread to go bust. Everybody would simply develop new tastes and eat more. I can be wealthy without your becoming poor; I can be obese without your dying of hunger. The entire global pie can grow.

Over the last 500 years the idea of progress convinced people to put more and more trust in the future. This trust created credit; credit brought real economic growth; and growth strengthened the trust in the future and opened the way for even more credit. It didn't happen overnight – the economy behaved more like a roller coaster than a balloon. But over the long run, with the bumps evened out, the general direction was unmistakable. Today, there is so much credit in the world that governments, business corporations and private individuals easily obtain *large, long-term and low-interest loans* that far exceed current income.

The belief in the growing global pie eventually turned revolutionary. In 1776 the Scottish economist Adam Smith published *The Wealth of Nations*, probably the most important economics manifesto of all time. In the eighth chapter of its first volume, Smith made the following novel argument: when a landlord, a weaver or a shoemaker has greater profits than he needs to maintain his own family, he uses the surplus to employ more assistants, in order to further increase his profits. The more profits he has, the more assistants he can employ. It follows that an increase in the profits of private entrepreneurs is the basis for the increase in collective wealth and prosperity.

This may not strike you as very original, because we all live in a capitalist world that takes Smith's argument for granted. We hear variations on this theme every day in the news. Yet Smith's claim that the selfish human urge to increase private profits is the basis for collective wealth is one of the most revolutionary ideas in human history – revolutionary not just from an economic perspective, but even more so from a moral and political perspective. What Smith says is, in fact, that greed is good, and that by becoming richer I benefit everybody, not just myself. *Egoism is altruism.*

Smith taught people to think about the economy as a 'win-win situation', in which my profits are also your profits. Not only can we both enjoy a bigger slice of pie at the same time, but the increase in your slice depends upon the increase in my slice. If I am poor, you too will be poor since I cannot buy your products or services. If I am rich, you too will be enriched since you can now sell me something. Smith denied the traditional contradiction between wealth and morality, and threw open the gates of heaven for the rich. Being rich meant being moral. In Smith's story, people become rich not by despoiling their neighbours, but by increasing the overall size of the pie. And when the pie grows, everyone benefits. The rich are accordingly the most useful and benevolent people in society, because they turn the wheels of growth for everyone's advantage.

All this depends, however, on the rich using their profits to open new factories and hire new employees, rather than wasting them on non-productive activities. Smith therefore repeated like a mantra the maxim that 'When profits increase, the landlord or weaver will employ more assistants' and not 'When profits increase, Scrooge will hoard his money in a chest and take it out only to count his coins.' A crucial part of the modern capitalist economy was the emergence of a new ethic, according to which profits ought to be reinvested in production. This brings about more profits, which are again reinvested in production, which brings more profits, et cetera ad infinitum.

Investments can be made in many ways: enlarging the factory, conducting scientific research, developing new products. Yet all these investments must somehow increase production and translate into larger profits. In the new capitalist creed, the first and most sacred commandment is: 'The profits of production must be reinvested in increasing production.'

That's why capitalism is called 'capitalism'. Capitalism distinguishes 'capital' from mere 'wealth'. Capital consists of money, goods and resources that are invested in production. Wealth, on the other hand, is buried in the ground or wasted on unproductive activities. A pharaoh who pours resources into a non-productive pyramid is not a capitalist. A pirate who loots a Spanish treasure fleet and buries a chest full of glittering coins on the beach of some Caribbean island is not a capitalist. But a hard-working factory hand who reinvests part of his income in the stock market is.

The idea that 'The profits of production must be reinvested in increasing production' sounds trivial. Yet it was alien to most people throughout history. In pre-modern times, people believed that the level of production was more or less constant. So why reinvest your profits if production won't increase by much, no matter what you do? Thus medieval noblemen espoused an ethic of generosity and conspicuous consumption. They spent their revenues on tournaments, banquets, palaces and wars, and on charity and monumental cathedrals. Few tried to reinvest profits in increasing their manors' output, developing better kinds of wheat, or looking for new markets.

In the modern era, the nobility has been overtaken by a new elite whose members are true believers in the capitalist creed. The new capitalist elite is made up not of dukes and marquises, but of board chairmen, stock traders and industrialists. These magnates are far richer than the medieval nobility, but they are far less interested in extravagant consumption, and they spend a much smaller part of their profits on non-productive activities.

Medieval noblemen wore colourful robes of gold and silk, and devoted much of their time to attending banquets, carnivals and glamorous tournaments. In comparison, modern CEOs don dreary uniforms called suits that afford them all the panache of a flock of crows, and they have little time for festivities. The typical venture capitalist rushes from one business meeting to another, trying to figure out where to invest his capital and following the ups and downs of the stocks and bonds he owns. True, his suits might be Versace and he might get to travel in a private jet, but these expenses are nothing compared to what he invests in increasing human production.

It's not just Versace-clad business moguls who invest to increase productivity. Ordinary folk and government agencies think along similar lines. How many dinner conversations in modest neighbourhoods sooner or later bog down in interminable debate about whether it is better to invest one's savings in the stock market, bonds or

How many dinner conversations in modest neighbourhoods sooner or later bog down in interminable debate about whether it is better to invest one's savings in the stock market, bonds or property?

property? Governments too strive to invest their tax revenues in productive enterprises that will increase future income – for example, building a new port could make it easier for factories to export their products, enabling them to make more taxable income, thereby increasing the government's future revenues. Another government might prefer to invest in education, on the grounds that educated people form the basis for the lucrative high-tech industries, which pay lots of taxes without needing extensive port facilities.

CAPITALISM BEGAN AS a theory about how the economy functions. It was both descriptive and prescriptive – it offered an account of how money worked and promoted the idea that reinvesting profits in production leads to fast economic growth. But capitalism gradually became far more than just an economic doctrine. It now encompasses an ethic – a set of teachings about how people should behave, educate their children and even think. Its principal tenet is that economic growth is the supreme good, or at least a proxy for the supreme good, because justice, freedom and even happiness all depend on economic growth. Ask a capitalist how to bring justice and political freedom to a place like Zimbabwe or Afghanistan, and you are likely to get a lecture on how economic affluence and a thriving middle class are essential for stable democratic institutions, and about the need therefore to inculcate in Afghan tribesmen the values of free enterprise, thrift and self-reliance.

This new religion has had a decisive influence on the development of modern science, too. Scientific research is usually funded by either governments or private businesses. When capitalist governments and businesses consider investing in a particular scientific project, the first questions are usually 'Will this project enable us to increase production and profits? Will it produce economic growth?' A project that can't clear these hurdles has little chance of finding a sponsor. No history of modern science can leave capitalism out of the picture.

Conversely, the history of capitalism is unintelligible without taking science into account. Capitalism's belief in perpetual economic growth flies in the face of almost everything we know about the universe. A society of wolves would be extremely foolish to believe that the supply of sheep would keep on growing indefinitely. The human economy has nevertheless managed to keep on growing throughout the modern era, thanks only to the fact that scientists come up with another discovery or gadget every few years – such as the continent of America, the internal combustion engine, or genetically engineered sheep. Banks and governments print money, but ultimately, it is the scientists who foot the bill.

Over the last few years, banks and governments have been frenziedly printing money. Everybody is terrified that the current economic crisis may stop the growth of the economy. So they are creating trillions of dollars, euros and yen out of thin air, pumping cheap credit into the system, and hoping that the scientists, technicians and engineers will manage to come up with something really big, before the bubble bursts. Everything depends on the people in the labs. New discoveries in fields such as biotechnology and nanotechnology could create entire new industries, whose profits could back the trillions of make-believe money that the banks and governments have created since 2008. If the labs do not fulfil these expectations before the bubble bursts, we are heading towards very rough times.

Columbus Searches for an Investor

CAPITALISM PLAYED A decisive role not only in the rise of modern science, but also in the emergence of European imperialism. And it was European imperialism that created the capitalist credit system in the first place. Of course, credit was not invented in modern Europe. It existed in almost all agricultural societies, and in the early modern period the emergence of European capitalism was closely linked to economic developments in Asia. Remember, too, that until the late eighteenth century, Asia was the world's economic powerhouse, meaning that Europeans had far less capital at their disposal than the Chinese, Muslims or Indians.

However, in the sociopolitical systems of China, India and the Muslim world, credit played only a secondary role. Merchants and bankers in the markets of Istanbul, Isfahan, Delhi and Beijing may have thought along capitalist lines, but the kings and generals in the palaces and forts tended to despise merchants and mercantile thinking. Most non-European empires of the early modern era were established by great conquerors such as Nurhaci and Nader Shah, or by bureaucratic and military elites as in the Qing and Ottoman empires. Financing wars through taxes and plunder (without making fine distinctions between the two), they owed little to credit systems, and they cared even less about the interests of bankers and investors.

In Europe, on the other hand, kings and generals gradually adopted the mercantile way of thinking, until merchants and bankers became the ruling elite. The European conquest of the world was increasingly financed through credit rather than taxes, and was increasingly directed by capitalists whose main ambition was to receive maximum returns on their investments. The empires built by bankers and merchants in frock coats and top hats defeated the empires built by kings and noblemen in gold clothes and shining armour. The mercantile empires were simply much shrewder in financing their conquests. Nobody wants to pay taxes, but everyone is happy to invest.

In 1484 Christopher Columbus approached the king of

Portugal with the proposal that he finance a fleet that would sail westward to find a new trade route to East Asia. Such explorations were a very risky and costly business. A lot of money was needed in order to build ships, buy supplies, and pay sailors and soldiers – and there was no guarantee that the investment would yield a return. The king of Portugal declined.

Like a present-day start-up entrepreneur, Columbus did not give up. He pitched his idea to other potential investors in Italy, France, England, and again in Portugal. Each time he was rejected. He then tried his luck with Ferdinand and Isabella, rulers of newly united Spain. He took on some experienced lobbyists, and with their help he managed to convince Queen Isabella to invest. As every school-child knows, Isabella hit the jackpot. Columbus' discoveries enabled the Spaniards to conquer America, where they established gold and silver mines as well as sugar and tobacco plantations that enriched the Spanish kings, bankers and merchants beyond their wildest dreams.

A hundred years later, princes and bankers were willing to extend far more credit to Columbus' successors, and they had more capital at their disposal, thanks to the treasures reaped from America. Equally important, princes and bankers had far more trust in the potential of exploration, and were more willing to part with their money. This was the magic circle of imperial capitalism: credit financed new discoveries; discoveries led to colonies; colonies provided profits; profits built trust; and trust translated into more credit. Nurhaci and Nader Shah ran out of fuel after a few thousand kilometres. Capitalist entrepreneurs only increased their financial momentum from conquest to conquest.

But these expeditions remained chancy affairs, so credit markets nevertheless remained quite cautious. Many expeditions returned to Europe empty-handed, having discovered nothing of value. The English, for instance, wasted a lot of capital in fruitless attempts to discover a north-western passage to Asia through the Arctic. Many other expeditions didn't return at all. Ships hit icebergs, foundered in tropical storms, or fell victim to pirates. In order to increase the number of potential investors and reduce the risk they incurred, Europeans turned to limited liability joint-stock companies. Instead of a single investor betting all his money on a single rickety ship, the joint-stock company collected money from a large number of investors, each risking only a small portion of his capital. The risks were thereby curtailed, but no cap was placed on the profits. Even a small investment in the right ship could turn you into a millionaire.

Decade by decade, western Europe witnessed the development of a sophisticated financial system that could raise large amounts of credit on short notice and put it at the disposal of private entrepreneurs and governments. This system could finance explorations and conquests far more efficiently than any kingdom or empire. The new-found power of credit can be seen in the bitter struggle between Spain and the Netherlands. In the sixteenth century, Spain was the most powerful state in Europe, holding sway over a vast global empire. It ruled much of Europe, huge chunks of North and South America, the Philippine Islands, and a string of bases along the coasts of Africa and Asia. Every year, fleets heavy with American and Asian treasures returned to the ports of Seville and Cadiz. The Netherlands was a small and windy swamp, devoid of natural resources, a small corner of the king of Spain's dominions.

In 1568 the Dutch, who were mainly Protestant, revolted against their Catholic Spanish overlord. At first the rebels seemed to play the role of Don Quixote, courageously tilting at invincible windmills. Yet within eighty years the Dutch had not only secured their independence from Spain, but had managed to replace the Spaniards and their Portuguese allies as masters of the ocean highways, build a global Dutch empire, and become the richest state in Europe.

The secret of Dutch success was credit. The Dutch burghers, who had little taste for combat on land, hired mercenary armies to fight the Spanish for them. The Dutch themselves meanwhile took to the sea in ever-larger fleets. Mercenary armies and cannon-brandishing fleets cost a fortune, but the Dutch were able to finance their military expeditions more easily than the mighty Spanish Empire because they secured the trust of the burgeoning European financial system at a time when the

Spanish king was carelessly eroding its trust in him. Financiers extended the Dutch enough credit to set up armies and fleets, and these armies and fleets gave the Dutch control of world trade routes, which in turn yielded handsome profits. The profits allowed the Dutch to repay the loans, which strengthened the trust of the financiers. Amsterdam was fast becoming not only one of the most important ports of Europe, but also the continent's financial Mecca.

How exactly did the Dutch win the trust of the financial system? Firstly, they were sticklers about repaying their loans on time and in full, making the extension of credit less risky for lenders. Secondly, their country's judicial system enjoyed independence and protected private rights – in particular private property rights. Capital trickles away from dictatorial states that fail to defend private individuals and their property. Instead, it flows into states upholding the rule of law and private property.

Imagine that you are the son of a solid family of German financiers. Your father sees an opportunity to expand the business by opening branches in major European cities. He sends you to Amsterdam and your younger brother to Madrid, giving you each 10,000 gold coins to invest. Your brother lends his start-up capital at interest to the king of Spain, who needs it to raise an army to fight the king of France. You decide to lend yours to a Dutch

merchant, who wants to invest in scrubland on the south-
ern end of a desolate island called Manhattan, certain
that property values there will skyrocket as the Hudson
River turns into a major trade artery. Both loans are to be
repaid within a year.

The year passes. The Dutch merchant sells the land
he's bought at a handsome markup and repays your money
with the interest he promised. Your father is pleased. But
your little brother in Madrid is getting nervous. The war
with France ended well for the king of Spain, but he has
now embroiled himself in a conflict with the Turks. He
needs every penny to finance the new war, and thinks this
is far more important than repaying old debts. Your
brother sends letters to the palace and asks friends with
connections at court to intercede, but to no avail. Not
only has your brother not earned the promised interest –
he's lost the principal. Your father is not pleased.

Now, to make matters worse, the king sends a treasury
official to your brother to tell him, in no uncertain terms,
that he expects to receive another loan of the same size,
forthwith. Your brother has no money to lend. He writes
home to dad, trying to persuade him that this time the
king will come through. The paterfamilias has a soft spot
for his youngest, and agrees with a heavy heart. Another
10,000 gold coins disappear into the Spanish treasury,
never to be seen again. Meanwhile in Amsterdam, things
are looking bright. You make more and more loans to
enterprising Dutch merchants, who repay them promptly

and in full. But your luck does not hold indefinitely. One of your usual clients has a hunch that wooden clogs are going to be the next fashion craze in Paris, and asks you for a loan to set up a footwear emporium in the French capital. You lend him the money, but unfortunately the clogs don't catch on with the French ladies, and the disgruntled merchant refuses to repay the loan.

Your father is furious, and tells both of you it is time to unleash the lawyers. Your brother files suit in Madrid against the Spanish monarch, while you file suit in Amsterdam against the erstwhile wooden-shoe wizard. In Spain, the law courts are subservient to the king – the judges serve at his pleasure and fear punishment if they do not do his will. In the Netherlands, the courts are a separate branch of government, not dependent on the country's burghers and princes. The court in Madrid throws out your brother's suit, while the court in Amsterdam finds in your favour and puts a lien on the clog-merchant's assets to force him to pay up. Your father has learned his lesson. Better to do business with merchants than with kings, and better to do it in Holland than in Madrid.

And your brother's travails are not over. The king of Spain desperately needs more money to pay his army. He's sure that your father has cash to spare. So he brings trumped-up treason charges against your brother. If he doesn't come up with 20,000 gold coins forthwith, he'll get cast into a dungeon and rot there until he dies.

Your father has had enough. He pays the ransom for his

beloved son, but swears never to do business in Spain again. He closes his Madrid branch and relocates your brother to Rotterdam. Two branches in Holland now look like a really good idea. He hears that even Spanish capitalists are smuggling their fortunes out of their country. They, too, realise that if they want to keep their money and use it to gain more wealth, they are better off investing it where the rule of law prevails and where private property is respected – in the Netherlands, for example.

In such ways did the king of Spain squander the trust of investors at the same time that Dutch merchants gained their confidence. And it was the Dutch merchants – not the Dutch state – who built the Dutch Empire. The king of Spain kept on trying to finance and maintain his conquests by raising unpopular taxes from a disgruntled populace. The Dutch merchants financed conquest by getting loans, and increasingly also by selling shares in their companies that entitled their holders to receive a portion of the company's profits. Cautious investors who would never have given their money to the king of Spain, and who would have thought twice before extending credit to the Dutch government, happily invested fortunes in the Dutch joint-stock companies that were the mainstay of the new empire.

If you thought a company was going to make a big profit but it had already sold all its shares, you could buy some from people who owned them, probably for a higher price than they originally paid. If you bought shares and later discovered that the company was in dire straits, you could try to unload your stock for a lower price. The resulting trade in company shares led to the establishment in most major European cities of stock exchanges, places where the shares of companies were traded.

The most famous Dutch joint-stock company, the Vereenigde Oostindische Compagnie, or VOC for short, was chartered in 1602, just as the Dutch were throwing off Spanish rule and the boom of Spanish artillery could still be heard not far from Amsterdam's ramparts. VOC used the money it raised from selling shares to build ships, send them to Asia, and bring back Chinese, Indian and Indonesian goods. It also financed military actions taken by company ships against competitors and pirates. Eventually VOC money financed the conquest of Indonesia.

Indonesia is the world's biggest archipelago. Its thousands upon thousands of islands were ruled in the early seventeenth century by hundreds of kingdoms, principalities, sultanates and tribes. When VOC merchants first arrived in Indonesia in 1603, their aims were strictly commercial. However, in order to secure their commercial interests and maximise the profits of the shareholders, VOC merchants began to fight against local potentates who charged inflated tariffs, as well as against European competitors. VOC armed its merchant ships with cannons; it recruited European, Japanese, Indian and Indonesian mercenaries; and it built forts and conducted full-scale battles and sieges. This enterprise may sound a little strange to us, but in the early modern age it was common for private companies to hire not only soldiers, but also generals and admirals, cannons and ships, and even entire off-the-shelf armies. The international community took this for granted and didn't raise an eyebrow when a private company established an empire.

Island after island fell to VOC mercenaries and a large part of Indonesia became a VOC colony. VOC ruled Indonesia for close to 200 years. Only in 1800 did the Dutch state assume control of Indonesia, making it a Dutch national colony for the following 150 years. Today some people warn that twenty-first-century corporations are accumulating too much power. Early modern history shows just how far that can go if businesses are allowed to pursue their self-interest unchecked.

While VOC operated in the Indian Ocean, the Dutch West Indies Company, or WIC, plied the Atlantic. In order to control trade on the important Hudson River, WIC built a settlement called New Amsterdam on an island at the river's mouth. The colony was threatened by Indians and repeatedly attacked by the British, who eventually captured it in 1664. The British changed its name to New York. The remains of the wall built by WIC to defend its colony against Indians and British are today paved over by the world's most famous street – Wall Street.

AS THE SEVENTEENTH century wound to an end, complacency and costly continental wars caused the Dutch to lose not only New York, but also their place as Europe's financial and imperial engine. The vacancy was hotly contested by France and Britain. At first France seemed to be in a far stronger position. It was bigger than Britain, richer, more populous, and it possessed a larger and more experienced army. Yet Britain managed to win the trust of the financial system whereas France proved itself unworthy. The behaviour of the French crown was particularly notorious during what was called the Mississippi Bubble, the largest financial crisis of eighteenth-century Europe. That story also begins with an empire-building joint-stock company.

In 1717 the Mississippi Company, chartered in France, set out to colonise the lower Mississippi valley, establishing the city of New Orleans in the process. To finance its ambitious plans, the company, which had good connections at the court of King Louis XV, sold shares on the Paris stock exchange. John Law, the company's director, was also the governor of the central bank of France. Furthermore, the king had appointed him controller-general of finances, an office roughly equivalent to that of a modern finance minister. In 1717 the lower Mississippi valley offered few attractions besides swamps and alligators, yet the Mississippi Company spread tales of fabulous riches and boundless opportunities. French aristocrats, businessmen and the stolid members of the urban bourgeoisie fell for these fantasies, and Mississippi share prices skyrocketed. Initially, shares were offered at 500 livres apiece. On 1 August 1719, shares traded at 2,750 livres. By 30 August, they were worth 4,100 livres, and on 4 September, they reached 5,000 livres. On 2 December the price of a Mississippi share crossed the threshold of 10,000 livres. Euphoria swept the streets of Paris. People sold all their possessions and took huge loans in order to buy Mississippi shares. Everybody believed they'd discovered the easy way to riches.

A few days later, the panic began. Some speculators realised that the share prices were totally unrealistic and unsustainable. They figured that they had better sell while stock prices were at their peak. As the supply of shares available rose, their price declined. When other investors saw the price going down, they also wanted to get out quick. The stock price plummeted further, setting off an avalanche. In order to stabilise prices, the central bank of France – at the direction of its governor, John Law – bought up Mississippi shares, but it could not do so for ever. Eventually it ran out of money. When this happened, the controller-general of finances, the same John Law, authorised the printing of more money in order to buy additional shares. This placed the entire French financial system inside the bubble. And not even this financial wizardry could save the day. The price of Mississippi shares dropped from 10,000 livres back to 1,000 livres, and then collapsed completely, and the shares lost every sou of their worth. By now, the central bank and the royal treasury owned a huge amount of worthless stock and had no money. The big speculators emerged largely unscathed – they had sold in time. Small investors lost everything, and many committed suicide.

The Mississippi Bubble was one of history's most spectacular financial crashes. The royal French financial system never recuperated fully from the blow. The way in which the Mississippi Company used its political clout to manipulate share prices and fuel the buying frenzy caused the public to lose faith in the French banking system and in the financial wisdom of the French king. Louis XV found it more and more difficult to raise credit. This became one of the chief reasons that the overseas French Empire fell into British hands. While the British could borrow money easily and at low interest rates, France had difficulties securing loans, and had to pay high interest on them. In order to finance his growing debts, the king of France borrowed more and more money at higher and higher interest rates. Eventually, in the 1780s, Louis XVI, who had ascended the throne on his grandfather's death, realised that half his annual budget was tied to servicing the interest on his loans, and that he was heading towards bankruptcy. Reluctantly, in 1789, Louis XVI convened the Estates General, the French parliament that had not met for a century and a half, in order to find a solution to the crisis. Thus began the French Revolution.

While the French overseas empire was crumbling, the British Empire was expanding rapidly. Like the Dutch Empire before it, the British Empire was established and run largely by private joint-stock companies based in the London stock exchange. The first English settlements in North America were established in the early seventeenth century by joint-stock companies such as the London Company, the Plymouth Company, the Dorchester Company and the Massachusetts Company.

The Indian subcontinent too was conquered not by the British state, but by the mercenary army of the British East India Company. This company outperformed even the VOC. From its headquarters in Leadenhall Street, London, it ruled a mighty Indian empire for about a century, maintaining a huge military force of up to 350,000 soldiers, considerably outnumbering the armed forces of the British monarchy. Only in 1858 did the British crown nationalise India along with the company's private army. Napoleon made fun of the British, calling them a nation of shopkeepers. Yet these shopkeepers defeated Napoleon himself, and their empire was the largest the world has ever seen.

In the Name of Capital

THE NATIONALISATION OF Indonesia by the Dutch crown (1800) and of India by the British crown (1858) hardly ended the embrace of capitalism and empire. On the contrary, the connection only grew stronger during the nineteenth century. Joint-stock companies no longer needed to establish and govern private colonies – their managers and large shareholders now pulled the strings of power in London, Amsterdam and Paris, and they could count on the state to look after their interests. As Marx and other social critics quipped, Western governments were becoming a capitalist trade union.

The most notorious example of how governments did the bidding of big money was the First Opium War, fought between Britain and China (1840–42). In the first half of the nineteenth century, the British East India Company and sundry British business people made fortunes by exporting drugs, particularly opium, to China. Millions of Chinese became addicts, debilitating the country both economically and socially. In the late 1830s the Chinese government issued a ban on drug trafficking, but British drug merchants simply ignored the law. Chinese authorities began to confiscate and destroy drug cargos. The drug cartels had close connections in Westminster and Downing Street – many MPs and Cabinet ministers in fact held stock in the drug companies – so they pressured the government to take action.

In 1840 Britain duly declared war on China in the name of 'free trade'. It was a walkover. The overconfident Chinese were no match for Britain's new wonder weapons – steamboats, heavy artillery, rockets and rapid-fire rifles. Under the subsequent peace treaty, China agreed not to constrain the activities of British drug merchants and to compensate them for damages inflicted by the Chinese police. Furthermore, the British demanded and received control of Hong Kong, which they proceeded to use as a secure base for drug trafficking (Hong Kong remained in British hands until 1997). In the late nineteenth century, about 40 million Chinese, a tenth of the country's population, were opium addicts.

Egypt, too, learned to respect the long arm of British capitalism. During the nineteenth century, French and British investors lent huge sums to the rulers of Egypt, first in order to finance the Suez Canal project, and later to fund far less successful enterprises. Egyptian debt swelled, and European creditors increasingly meddled in Egyptian affairs. In 1881 Egyptian nationalists had had enough and rebelled. They declared a unilateral abrogation of all foreign debt. Queen Victoria was not amused. A year later she dispatched her army and navy to the Nile and Egypt remained a British protectorate until after the Second World War.

THESE WERE HARDLY the only wars fought in the interests of investors. In fact, war itself could become a commodity, just like opium. In 1821 the Greeks rebelled against the Ottoman Empire. The uprising aroused great sympathy in liberal and romantic circles in Britain – Lord Byron, the poet, even went to Greece to fight alongside the insurgents. But London financiers saw an opportunity as well. They proposed to the rebel leaders the issue of tradable Greek Rebellion Bonds on the London stock exchange. The Greeks would promise to repay the bonds, plus interest, if and when they won their independence. Private investors bought bonds to make a profit, or out of sympathy for the Greek cause, or both. The value of Greek Rebellion Bonds rose and fell on the London stock exchange in tempo with military successes and failures on the battlefields of Hellas. The Turks gradually gained the upper hand. With a rebel defeat imminent, the bond-holders faced the prospect of losing their trousers. The bondholders' interest was the national interest, so the British organised an international fleet that, in 1827, sank the main Ottoman flotilla in the Battle of Navarino. After centuries of subjugation, Greece was finally free. But freedom came with a huge debt that the new country had no way of repaying. The Greek economy was mortgaged to British creditors for decades to come.

The bear hug between capital and politics has had far-reaching implications for the credit market. The amount of credit in an economy is determined not only by purely economic factors such as the discovery of a new oil field or the invention of a new machine, but also by political events such as regime changes or more ambitious foreign policies. After the Battle of Navarino, British capitalists were more willing to invest their money in risky overseas deals. They had seen that if a foreign debtor refused to repay loans, Her Majesty's army would get their money back.

This is why today a country's credit rating is far more important to its economic well-being than are its natural resources. Credit ratings indicate the probability that a country will pay its debts. In addition to purely economic data, they take into account political, social and even cultural factors. An oil-rich country cursed with a despotic government, endemic warfare and a corrupt judicial system will usually receive a low credit rating. As a result, it is likely to remain relatively poor since it will not be able to raise the necessary capital to make the most of its oil bounty. A country devoid of natural resources, but which enjoys peace, a fair judicial system and a free government is likely to receive a high credit rating. As such, it may be able to raise enough cheap capital to support a good education system and foster a flourishing high-tech industry.

The Cult of the Free Market

CAPITAL AND POLITICS influence each other to such an extent that their relations are hotly debated by economists, politicians and the general public alike. Ardent capitalists tend to argue that capital should be free to influence politics, but politics should not be allowed to influence capital. They argue that when governments interfere in the markets, political interests cause them to make unwise investments that result in slower growth. For example, a government may impose heavy taxation on industrialists and use the money to give lavish unemployment benefits, which are popular with voters. In the view of many business people, it would be far better if the government left the money with them. They would use it, they claim, to open new factories and hire the unemployed.

In this view, the wisest economic policy is to keep politics out of the economy, reduce taxation and government regulation to a minimum, and allow market forces free rein to take their course. Private investors, unencumbered by political considerations, will invest their money where they can get the most profit, so the way to ensure the most economic growth – which will benefit everyone, industrialists and workers – is for the government to do as little as possible. This free-market doctrine is today the most common and influential variant of the capitalist creed. The most enthusiastic advocates of the free market criticise military adventures abroad with as much zeal as welfare programmes at home. They offer governments the same advice that Zen masters offer initiates: just do nothing.

But in its extreme form, belief in the free market is as naive as belief in Santa Claus. There simply is no such thing as a market free of all political bias. The most important economic resource is trust in the future, and this resource is constantly threatened by thieves and charlatans. Markets by themselves offer no protection against fraud, theft and violence. It is the job of political systems to ensure trust by legislating sanctions against cheats and to establish and support police forces, courts and jails which will enforce the law. When kings fail to do

In its extreme form, belief in the free market is as naive as belief in Santa Claus.

their jobs and regulate the markets properly, it leads to loss of trust, dwindling credit and economic depression. That was the lesson taught by the Mississippi Bubble of 1719, and anyone who forgot it was reminded by the US housing bubble of 2007, and the ensuing credit crunch and recession.

The Capitalist Hell

THERE IS AN even more fundamental reason why it's dangerous to give markets a completely free rein. Adam Smith taught that the shoemaker would use his surplus to employ more assistants. This implies that egoistic greed is beneficial for all, since profits are utilised to expand production and hire more employees.

Yet what happens if the greedy shoemaker increases his profits by paying employees less and increasing their work hours? The standard answer is that the free market would protect the employees. If our shoemaker pays too little and demands too much, the best employees would naturally abandon him and go to work for his competitors. The tyrant shoemaker would find himself left with the worst labourers, or with no labourers at all. He would have to mend his ways or go out of business. His own greed would compel him to treat his employees well.

This sounds bulletproof in theory, but in practice the bullets get through all too easily. In a completely free market, unsupervised by kings and priests, avaricious capitalists can establish monopolies or collude against their workforces. If there is a single corporation controlling all shoe factories in a country, or if all factory owners conspire to reduce wages simultaneously, then the labourers are no longer able to protect themselves by switching jobs.

Even worse, greedy bosses might curtail the workers' freedom of movement through debt peonage or slavery. At the end of the Middle Ages, slavery was almost unknown in Christian Europe. During the early modern period, the rise of European capitalism went hand in hand with the rise of the Atlantic slave trade. Unrestrained market forces, rather than tyrannical kings or racist ideologues, were responsible for this calamity.

When the Europeans conquered America, they opened gold and silver mines and established sugar, tobacco and cotton plantations. These mines and plantations became the mainstay of American production and export. The sugar plantations were particularly important. In the Middle Ages, sugar was a rare luxury in Europe. It was imported from the Middle East at prohibitive prices and used sparingly as a secret ingredient in delicacies and snake-oil medicines. After large sugar plantations were established in America, ever-increasing amounts of sugar began to reach Europe. The price of sugar dropped and Europe developed an insatiable sweet tooth. Entrepreneurs met this need by producing huge quantities of sweets: cakes, cookies, chocolate, candy, and sweetened beverages such as cocoa, coffee and tea. The annual sugar intake of the average Englishman rose from near zero in the early seventeenth century to around eight kilograms in the early nineteenth century.

However, growing cane and extracting its sugar was a labour-intensive business. Few people wanted to work long hours in malaria-infested sugar fields under a tropical sun. Contract labourers would have produced a commodity too expensive for mass consumption. Sensitive to market forces, and greedy for profits and economic growth, European plantation owners switched to slaves.

From the sixteenth to the nineteenth centuries, about 10 million African slaves were imported to America. About 70 per cent of them worked on the sugar plantations. Labour conditions were abominable. Most slaves lived a short and miserable life, and millions more died during wars waged to capture slaves or during the long voyage from inner Africa to the shores of America. All this so that Europeans could enjoy their sweet tea and candy – and sugar barons could enjoy huge profits.

The slave trade was not controlled by any state or government. It was a purely economic enterprise, organised and financed by the free market according to the laws of supply and demand. Private slave-trading companies sold shares on the Amsterdam, London and Paris stock exchanges. Middle-class Europeans looking for a good investment bought these shares. Relying on this money, the companies bought ships, hired sailors and soldiers, purchased slaves in Africa, and transported them to America. There they sold the slaves to the plantation owners, using the proceeds to purchase plantation products such as sugar, cocoa, coffee, tobacco, cotton and rum. They returned to Europe, sold the sugar and cotton for a good price, and then sailed to Africa to begin another round. The shareholders were very pleased with this arrangement. Throughout the eighteenth century the yield on slave-trade investments was about 6 per cent a year – they were extremely profitable, as any modern consultant would be quick to admit.

This is the fly in the ointment of free-market capitalism. It cannot ensure that profits are gained in a fair way, or distributed in a fair manner. On the contrary, the craving to increase profits and production blinds people to anything that might stand in the way. When growth becomes a supreme good, unrestricted by any other ethical considerations, it can easily lead to catastrophe. Some religions, such as Christianity and Nazism, have killed millions out of burning hatred. Capitalism has killed millions out of cold indifference coupled with greed. The Atlantic slave trade did not stem from racist hatred towards Africans. The individuals who bought the shares, the brokers who sold them, and the managers of the slave-trade companies rarely thought about the Africans. Nor did the owners of the sugar plantations. Many owners lived far from their plantations, and the only information they demanded were neat ledgers of profits and losses.

It is important to remember that the Atlantic slave trade was not a single aberration in an otherwise spotless record. The Great Bengal Famine was caused by a similar dynamic – the British East India Company cared more about its profits than about the lives of 10 million Bengalis. VOC's military campaigns in Indonesia were financed by upstanding Dutch burghers who loved their children, gave to charity, and enjoyed good music and fine art, but had no regard for the suffering of the inhabitants of Java, Sumatra and Malacca. Countless other crimes and misdemeanours accompanied the growth of the modern economy in other parts of the planet.

THE NINETEENTH CENTURY brought no improvement in the ethics of capitalism. The Industrial Revolution that swept through Europe enriched the bankers and capital-owners, but condemned millions of workers to a life of abject poverty. In the European colonies things were even worse. In 1876, King Leopold II of Belgium set up a non-governmental humanitarian organisation with the declared aim of exploring Central Africa and fighting the slave trade along the Congo River. It was also charged with improving conditions for the inhabitants of the region by building roads, schools and hospitals. In 1885 the European powers agreed to give this organisation control of 2.3 million square kilometres in the Congo basin. This territory, seventy-five times the size of Belgium, was henceforth known as the Congo Free State.

Nobody asked the opinion of the territory's 20–30 million inhabitants.

Within a short time the humanitarian organisation became a business enterprise whose real aim was growth and profit. The schools and hospitals were forgotten, and the Congo basin was instead filled with mines and plantations, run by mostly Belgian officials who ruthlessly exploited the local population. The rubber industry was particularly notorious. Rubber was fast becoming an industrial staple, and rubber export was the Congo's most important source of income. The African villagers who collected the rubber were required to provide higher and higher quotas. Those who failed to deliver their quota were punished brutally for their 'laziness'. Their arms were chopped off and occasionally entire villages were massacred. According to the most moderate estimates, between 1885 and 1908 the pursuit of growth and profits cost the lives of 6 million individuals (at least 20 per cent of the Congo's population). Some estimates reach up to 10 million deaths.

After 1908, and especially after 1945, capitalist greed was somewhat reined in, not least due to the fear of Communism. Yet inequities are still rampant. The economic pie of 2014 is far larger than the pie of 1500, but it is distributed so unevenly that many African peasants and Indonesian labourers return home after a hard day's work with less food than did their ancestors 500 years ago. Much like the Agricultural Revolution, so too the growth of the modern economy might turn out to be a colossal fraud. The human species and the global economy may well keep growing, but many more individuals may live in hunger and want.

Capitalism has two answers to this criticism. First, capitalism has created a world that nobody but a capitalist is capable of running. The only serious attempt to manage the world differently – Communism – was so much worse in almost every conceivable way that nobody has the stomach to try again. In 8500 BC one could cry bitter tears over the Agricultural Revolution, but it was too late to give up agriculture. Similarly, we may not like capitalism, but we cannot live without it.

The second answer is that we just need more patience – paradise, the capitalists promise, is right around the corner. True, mistakes have been made, such as the Atlantic slave trade and the exploitation of the European working class. But we have learned our lesson, and if we just wait a little longer and allow the pie to grow a little bigger, everybody will receive a fatter slice. The division of spoils will never be equitable, but there will be enough to satisfy every man, woman and child – even in the Congo.

There are, indeed, some positive signs. At least when we use purely material criteria – such as life expectancy, child mortality and calorie intake – the standard of living of the average human in 2014 is significantly higher than it was in 1914, despite the exponential growth in the number of humans.

Yet can the economic pie grow indefinitely? Every pie requires raw materials and energy. Prophets of doom warn that sooner or later *Homo sapiens* will exhaust the raw materials and energy of planet Earth. And what will happen then?

The Great Decoupling

LIBERALS UPHOLD FREE markets and democratic elections because they believe that every human is a uniquely valuable individual, whose free choices are the ultimate source of authority. In the twenty-first century three *practical* developments might make this belief obsolete:

1. Humans will lose their economic and military usefulness, hence the economic and political system will stop attaching much value to them.
2. The system will continue to find value in humans collectively, but not in unique individuals.
3. The system will still find value in some unique individuals, but these will constitute a new elite of upgraded superhumans rather than the mass of the population.

Let's examine all three threats in detail. The first – that technological developments will make humans economically and militarily useless – will not prove that liberalism is wrong on a philosophical level, but in practice it is hard to see how democracy, free markets and other liberal institutions can survive such a blow. After all, liberalism did not become the dominant ideology simply because its philosophical arguments were the most valid. Rather, liberalism succeeded because there was abundant political, economic and military sense in ascribing value to every human being. On the mass battlefields of modern industrial wars and in the mass production lines of modern industrial economies, every human counted. There was value to every pair of hands that could hold a rifle or pull a lever.

In the spring of 1793 the royal houses of Europe sent their armies to strangle the French Revolution in its cradle. The firebrands in Paris reacted by proclaiming the *levée en masse* and unleashing the first total war. On 23 August the National Convention decreed that 'From this moment until such time as its enemies shall have been driven from the soil of the Republic, all Frenchmen are in permanent requisition for the services of the armies. The young men shall fight; the married men shall forge arms and transport provisions; the women shall make tents and clothes and shall serve in the hospitals; the children shall turn old lint into linen; and the old men shall betake themselves to the public squares in order to arouse the courage of the warriors and preach hatred of kings and the unity of the Republic.'

This decree sheds interesting light on the French

Revolution's most famous document – *The Declaration of the Rights of Man and of the Citizen* – which recognised that all citizens have equal value and equal political rights. Is it a coincidence that universal rights were proclaimed at the precise historical juncture when universal conscription was decreed? Though scholars may quibble about the exact relations between them, in the following two centuries a common argument in defence of democracy explained that giving citizens political rights is good, because the soldiers and workers of democratic countries perform better than those of dictatorships. Allegedly, granting political rights to people increases their motivation and their initiative, which is useful both on the battlefield and in the factory.

Thus Charles W. Eliot, president of Harvard from 1869 to 1909, wrote on 5 August 1917 in the *New York Times* that 'democratic armies fight better than armies aristocratically organised and autocratically governed' and that 'the armies of nations in which the mass of the people determine legislation, elect their public servants, and settle questions of peace and war, fight better than the armies of an autocrat who rules by right of birth and by commission from the Almighty'.

A similar rationale favoured the enfranchisement of women in the wake of the First World War. Realising the vital role of women in total industrial wars, countries saw the need to give them political rights in peacetime. Thus in 1918 President Woodrow Wilson became a supporter of women's suffrage, explaining to the US Senate that the First World War 'could not have been fought, either by the other nations engaged or by America, if it had not been for the services of women – services rendered in every sphere – not only in the fields of effort in which we have been accustomed to see them work, but wherever men have worked and upon the very skirts and edges of the battle itself. We shall not only be distrusted but shall deserve to be distrusted if we do not enfranchise them with the fullest possible enfranchisement.'

However, in the twenty-first century the majority of both men and women might lose their military and economic value. Gone is the mass conscription of the two world wars. The most advanced armies of the twenty-first century rely far more on cutting-edge technology. Instead of limitless cannon fodder, countries now need only small numbers of highly trained soldiers, even smaller numbers of special forces super-warriors and a handful of experts who know how to produce and use sophisticated technology. Hi-tech forces 'manned' by pilotless drones and cyber-worms are replacing the mass armies of the twentieth century, and generals delegate more and more critical decisions to algorithms.

Aside from their unpredictability and their susceptibility to fear, hunger and fatigue, flesh-and-blood soldiers think and move on an increasingly irrelevant timescale. From the days of Nebuchadnezzar to those of Saddam Hussein, despite myriad technological improvements, war was waged on an organic timetable. Discussions lasted for hours, battles took days, and wars dragged on for years. Cyber-wars, however, may last just a few minutes. When a lieutenant on shift at cyber-command notices something odd is going on, she picks up the phone to call her superior, who immediately alerts the White House. Alas, by the time the president reaches for the red handset, the war has already been lost. Within seconds a sufficiently sophisticated cyber strike might shut down the US power grid, wreck US flight control centres, cause numerous industrial accidents in nuclear plants and chemical installations, disrupt the police, army and intelligence communication networks – and wipe out financial records so that trillions of dollars simply vanish without a trace and nobody knows who owns what. The only thing curbing public hysteria is that, with the Internet, television and radio down, people will not be aware of the full magnitude of the disaster.

On a smaller scale, suppose two drones fight each other in the air. One drone cannot open fire without first receiving the go-ahead from a human operator in some distant bunker. The other is fully autonomous. Which drone do you think will prevail? If in 2093 the decrepit European Union sends its drones and cyborgs to snuff out a new French Revolution, the Paris Commune might press into service every available hacker, computer and smartphone, but it will have little use for most humans, except perhaps as human shields. It is telling that already today in many asymmetrical conflicts the majority of citizens are reduced to serving as human shields for advanced armaments.

Even if you care more about justice than victory, you should probably opt to replace your soldiers and pilots with autonomous robots and drones. Human soldiers murder, rape and pillage, and even when they try to behave themselves, they all too often kill civilians by mistake. Computers programmed with ethical algorithms could far more easily conform to the latest rulings of the international criminal court.

In the economic sphere too, the ability to hold a hammer or press a button is becoming less valuable than before, which endangers the critical alliance between liberalism and capitalism. In the twentieth century liberals explained that we don't have to choose between ethics and economics. Protecting human rights and liberties was both a moral imperative and the key to economic growth. Britain, France and the United States allegedly prospered because they liberalised their economies and societies, and if Turkey, Brazil or China wanted to become equally prosperous, they had to do the same. In many if not most cases it was the economic rather than the moral argument that convinced tyrants and juntas to liberalise.

In the twenty-first century liberalism will have a much harder time selling itself. As the masses lose their economic importance, will the moral argument alone be enough to protect human rights and liberties? Will elites and governments go on valuing every human being even when it pays no economic dividends?

In the past there were many things only humans could do. But now robots and computers are catching up and may soon outperform humans in most tasks. True, computers function very differently from humans, and it seems unlikely that computers will become humanlike any time soon. In particular, it doesn't seem that computers are about to gain consciousness and start experiencing emotions and sensations. Over the past half-century there has been an immense advance in computer intelligence, but there has been exactly zero advance in computer consciousness. As far as we know, computers in 2016 are no more conscious than their prototypes in the 1950s. However, we are on the brink of a momentous revolution. Humans are in danger of losing their economic value, because intelligence is decoupling from consciousness.

Until today high intelligence always went hand in hand with a developed consciousness. Only conscious beings could perform tasks that required a lot of intelligence, such as playing chess, driving cars, diagnosing diseases or identifying terrorists. However, we are now developing new types of non-conscious intelligence that can perform such tasks far better than humans. For all these tasks are based on pattern recognition, and non-conscious algorithms may soon excel human consciousness in recognising patterns.

We are on the brink of a momentous revolution.

Science-fiction movies generally assume that in order to match and surpass human intelligence, computers will have to develop consciousness. But real science tells a different story. There might be several alternative ways leading to super-intelligence, only some of which pass through the straits of consciousness. For millions of years organic evolution has been slowly sailing along the conscious route. The evolution of inorganic computers may completely bypass these narrow straits, charting a different and much quicker course to super-intelligence.

This raises a novel question: which of the two is really important, intelligence or consciousness? As long as they went hand in hand, debating their relative value was just an amusing pastime for philosophers. But in the twenty-first century this is becoming an urgent political and economic issue. And it is sobering to realise that, at least for armies and corporations, the answer is straightforward: intelligence is mandatory but consciousness is optional.

Armies and corporations cannot function without intelligent agents, but they don't need consciousness and subjective experiences. The conscious experiences of a flesh-and-blood taxi driver are infinitely richer than those of a self-driving car, which feels absolutely nothing. The taxi driver can enjoy music while navigating the busy streets of Seoul. His mind may expand in awe as he looks up at the stars and contemplates the mysteries of the universe. His eyes may fill with tears of joy when he sees his baby girl taking her very first step. But the system doesn't need all that from a taxi driver. All it really wants is to bring passengers from point A to point B as quickly, safely and cheaply as possible. And the autonomous car will soon be able to do that far better than a human driver, even though it cannot enjoy music or be awestruck by the magic of existence.

We should remind ourselves of the fate of horses during the Industrial Revolution. An ordinary farm horse can smell, love, recognise faces, jump over fences and do a thousand other things far better than a Model T Ford or a million-dollar Lamborghini. But cars nevertheless replaced horses because they were superior in the handful of tasks that the system really needed. Taxi drivers are highly likely to go the way of horses.

Indeed, if we forbid humans to drive not only taxis but vehicles altogether, and give computer algorithms a monopoly over traffic, we can then connect all vehicles to a single network, thereby rendering car accidents far less likely. In August 2015 one of Google's experimental self-driving cars had an accident. As it approached a crossing and detected pedestrians wishing to cross, it applied its brakes. A moment later it was hit from behind by a sedan whose careless human driver was perhaps contemplating the mysteries of the universe instead of watching the road. This could not have happened if *both* vehicles had been guided by interlinked computers. The controlling algorithm would have known the position and intentions of every vehicle on the road, and would not have allowed two of its marionettes to collide. Such a system would save lots of time, money and human lives – but would also eliminate the human experience of driving a car and tens of millions of human jobs.

Some economists predict that sooner or later unenhanced humans will be completely useless. Robots and 3D printers are already replacing workers in manual jobs such as manufacturing shirts, and highly intelligent algorithms will do the same to white-collar occupations. Bank clerks and travel agents, who a short time ago seemed completely secure from automation, have become endangered species. How many travel agents do we need when we can use our smartphones to buy plane tickets from an algorithm?

Stock-exchange traders are also in danger. Most financial trading today is already being managed by computer algorithms that can process in a second more data than a human can in a year, and can react to the data much faster than a human can blink. On 23 April 2013, Syrian hackers broke into Associated Press's official Twitter account. At 13:07 they tweeted that the White House had been attacked and President Obama was hurt. Trade algorithms that constantly monitor newsfeeds reacted in no time and began selling stocks like mad. The Dow Jones went into free fall and within sixty seconds lost 150 points, equivalent to a loss of $136 billion! At 13:10 Associated Press clarified that the tweet was a hoax. The algorithms reversed gear and by 13:13 the Dow Jones had recuperated almost all the losses.

Three years earlier, on 6 May 2010, the New York stock exchange underwent an even sharper shock. Within five minutes – from 14:42 to 14:47 – the Dow Jones dropped by 1,000 points, wiping out $1 trillion. It then bounced back, returning to its pre-crash level in a little more than three minutes. That's what happens when super-fast computer programs are in charge of our money. Experts have been trying ever since to understand what happened in this so-called 'Flash Crash'. They know algorithms were to blame, but are still not sure exactly what went wrong. Some traders in the USA have already filed lawsuits against algorithmic trading, arguing that it unfairly discriminates against human beings who simply cannot react fast enough to compete. Quibbling whether this really constitutes a violation of rights might provide lots of work and lots of fees for lawyers.

And these lawyers won't necessarily be human. Movies and TV series give the impression that lawyers spend their days in court shouting 'Objection!' and making impassioned speeches. Yet most run-of-the-mill lawyers devote their time to perusing endless files, looking for precedents, loopholes and tiny pieces of potentially relevant evidence. Some are busy trying to figure out what happened on the night John Doe was murdered, or formulating a gargantuan business contract that will protect their client against every conceivable eventuality. What will be the fate of all these lawyers once sophisticated search algorithms can locate more precedents in a day than a human can in a lifetime, and once brain scans can reveal lies and deceptions at the press of a button? Even highly experienced lawyers and detectives cannot easily spot duplicity merely by observing people's facial expressions and tone of voice. However, lying involves different brain areas from those used in telling the truth. We're not there yet, but it is conceivable that in the not too distant future fMRI scanners could function as almost infallible truth machines. Where will that leave millions of lawyers, judges, cops and detectives? They might consider returning to school to learn a new profession.

When they enter the classroom, however, they may well discover that the algorithms have got there first. Companies such as Mindojo are developing interactive algorithms that will not only teach me maths, physics and history, but will simultaneously study me and get to know exactly who I am. Digital teachers will closely monitor every answer I give, and how long it took me to give it. Over time they will discern my unique weaknesses as well as my strengths and will identify what gets me excited and what makes my eyelids droop. They could teach me thermodynamics or geometry in a way that suits my personality type, even if that particular method doesn't suit 99 per cent of the other pupils. And these digital teachers will never lose their patience, never shout at me, and never go on strike. It remains unclear, however, why on earth I would need to know thermodynamics or geometry in a world containing such intelligent computer programs.

Even doctors are fair game for the algorithms. The first and foremost task of most doctors is to diagnose diseases correctly and then suggest the best available treatment. If I arrive at the clinic complaining of fever and diarrhoea, I might be suffering from food poisoning. Then again, the same symptoms might result from a stomach virus, cholera, dysentery, malaria, cancer or some unknown new disease. My physician has only a few minutes to make a correct diagnosis, because that is all the time my health insurance pays for. This allows for no more than a few questions and perhaps a quick medical examination. The doctor then cross-references this meagre information with my medical history, and with the vast world of human maladies. Alas, not even the most diligent doctor can remember all my previous ailments and check-ups. Similarly, no doctor can be familiar with every illness and drug, or read every new article published in every medical journal. To top it all, the doctor is sometimes tired or hungry or perhaps even sick, which affects her judgement. No wonder that doctors sometimes err in their diagnoses or recommend a less-than-optimal treatment.

Now consider IBM's famous Watson – an artificial intelligence system that won the *Jeopardy!* television game show in 2011, beating human former champions. Watson is currently groomed to do more serious work, particularly in diagnosing diseases. An AI such as Watson has enormous potential advantages over human doctors. Firstly, an AI can hold in its databanks information about every known illness and medicine in history. It can then update these databanks daily, not only with the findings of new researches, but also with medical statistics gathered from every linked-in clinic and hospital in the world.

Secondly, Watson will be intimately familiar not only with my entire genome and my day-to-day medical history, but also with the genomes and medical histories of my parents, siblings, cousins, neighbours and friends. Watson will know instantly whether I visited a tropical country recently, whether I have recurring stomach infections, whether there have been cases of intestinal cancer in my family or whether people all over town are complaining this morning about diarrhoea.

Thirdly, Watson will never be tired, hungry or sick, and will have all the time in the world for me. I could sit comfortably on my sofa at home and answer hundreds of questions, telling Watson exactly how I feel. This is good news for most patients (except perhaps hypochondriacs). But if you enter medical school today in the expectation of still being a family doctor in twenty years, maybe you should think again. With such a Watson around, there is not much need for Sherlocks.

This threat hovers over the heads not only of general practitioners, but also of experts. Indeed, it might prove easier to replace doctors specialising in relatively narrow fields such as cancer diagnosis. In a recent experiment a computer algorithm correctly diagnosed 90 per cent of lung cancer cases presented to it, while human doctors had a success rate of only 50 per cent. In fact, the future is already here. CT scans and mammography exams are routinely checked by specialised algorithms, which provide doctors with a second opinion, and sometimes detect tumours that the doctors missed.

A host of tough technical problems still prevent Watson and its ilk from displacing most doctors tomorrow morning. Yet these technical problems – however difficult – need only be solved once. The training of a human doctor is a complicated and expensive process that lasts years. When the process is complete, after a decade or so of studies and internships, all you get is one doctor. If you want two doctors, you have to repeat the entire process from scratch. In contrast, if and when you solve the technical problems hampering Watson, you will get not one, but an infinite number of doctors, available 24/7 in every corner of the world. So even if it costs $100 billion to make it work, in the long run it would be much cheaper than training human doctors.

Of course not all human doctors will disappear. Tasks that require a greater level of creativity than run-of-the-mill diagnosis will remain in human hands for the foreseeable future. Just as twenty-first-century armies are increasing the size of their elite special forces, so future healthcare services might offer many more openings to the medical equivalents of army rangers and navy SEALs. However, just as armies no longer need millions of GIs, so future health-care services will not need millions of GPs.

What's true of doctors is doubly true of pharmacists. In 2011 a pharmacy opened in San Francisco manned by a single robot. When a human comes to the pharmacy, within seconds the robot receives all of the customer's prescriptions, as well as detailed information about her suspected allergies and any other medicines she takes. In its first year of operation the robotic pharmacist provided 2 million prescriptions, without making a single mistake. On average, flesh-and-blood pharmacists err in 1.7 per cent of all prescriptions. In the United States alone this amounts to more than 50 million mistaken prescriptions every year!

Some people argue that even if an algorithm could out-perform doctors and pharmacists in the technical aspects of their professions, it could never replace their human touch. If your CT indicates you have cancer, would you prefer to receive the news from a cold machine or from a human doctor attentive to your emotional state? Well, how about receiving the news from an attentive machine that tailors its words to your feelings and personality type? Remember that organisms are algorithms, and Watson could detect your emotions with the same accuracy that it detects your tumours.

A human doctor recognises your emotional state by analysing external signals such as your facial expression and your tone of voice. Watson could not only analyse such external signals more accurately than a human doctor, but it could simultaneously analyse numerous internal indicators that are normally hidden from our eyes and ears. By monitoring your blood pressure, brain activities and countless other biometric data Watson could know exactly how you feel. Thanks to statistics garnered from millions of previous social encounters, Watson could then tell you precisely what you need to hear in just the right tone of voice. For all their vaunted emotional intelligence, human beings are often overwhelmed by their own emotions and react in counterproductive ways. For example, encountering an angry person they start shouting, and listening to a fearful person they let their own anxieties run wild. Watson would never succumb to such temptations. Having no emotions of its own, it would always offer the most appropriate response to your emotional state.

This idea has already been partly implemented by some customer-services departments, such as those pioneered by the Mattersight Corporation. Mattersight publishes its wares with the following blurb: 'Have you ever spoken with someone and felt as though you just clicked? The magical feeling you get is the result of a personality connection. Mattersight creates that feeling every day, in call centers around the world.' When you phone customer services with a request or complaint, Mattersight routes your call by a clever algorithm. You first state your reason for calling. The algorithm listens to your problem, analyses the words you have used and your tone of voice, and deduces not only your present emotional state but also your personality type – introverted, extroverted, rebellious or dependent. Based on this information the algorithm forwards your call to the representative who best matches your mood and personality. The algorithm knows whether you need an empathetic person to listen patiently to your complaints, or a no-nonsense rational type who will give you the quickest technical solution. A good match means both happier customers and less time and money wasted by the customer-service department.

The Useless Class

THE MOST IMPORTANT question in twenty-first-century economics may well be what to do with all the superfluous people. What will conscious humans do once we have highly intelligent non-conscious algorithms that can do almost everything better?

Throughout history the job market has been divided into three main sectors: agriculture, industry and services. Until about 1800 the vast majority of people worked in agriculture and only a small minority worked in industry and services. During the Industrial Revolution people in developed countries left the fields and flocks. Most began working in industry, but growing numbers also took up jobs in the services sector. In recent decades developed countries underwent another revolution: as industrial jobs vanished the services sector expanded. In 2010 only 2 per cent of Americans worked in agriculture and 20 per cent worked in industry, while 78 per cent worked as teachers, doctors, webpage designers and so forth. When mindless algorithms are able to teach, diagnose and design better than humans, what will we do?

This is not an entirely new question. Ever since the Industrial Revolution erupted, people feared that mechanisation might cause mass unemployment. This never happened, because as old professions became obsolete, new professions evolved, and there was always something humans could do better than machines. Yet this is not a law of nature, and nothing guarantees it will continue to be like that in the future. Humans have two basic types of abilities: physical and cognitive. As long as machines competed with us humans merely in physical abilities, there were countless cognitive tasks that humans perfomed better. So as machines took over purely manual jobs, humans focused on jobs requiring at least some cognitive skills. Yet what will happen once algorithms outperform us in remembering, analysing and recognising patterns?

The idea that humans will always have a unique ability beyond the reach of non-conscious algorithms is just wishful thinking. The current scientific answer to this pipe dream can be summarised in three simple principles:

1. Organisms are algorithms. Every animal – including *Homo sapiens* – is an assemblage of organic algorithms shaped by natural selection over millions of years of evolution.

2. Algorithmic calculations are not affected by the materials from which the calculator is built. Whether an abacus is made of wood, iron or plastic, two beads plus two beads equals four beads.

3. Hence there is no reason to think that organic algorithms can do things that non-organic algorithms will never be able to replicate or surpass. As long as the calculations remain valid, what does it matter whether the algorithms are manifested in carbon or silicon?

True, at present there are numerous things that organic algorithms do better than non-organic ones, and experts have repeatedly declared that something will 'for ever' remain beyond the reach of non-organic algorithms. But it turns out that 'for ever' often means no more than a decade or two. Until a short time ago facial recognition was a favourite example of something that even babies accomplish easily but which escaped even the most powerful computers. Today facial-recognition programs are able to identify people far more efficiently and quickly than humans can. Police forces and intelligence services now routinely use such programs to scan countless hours of video footage from surveillance cameras in order to track down suspects and criminals.

In the 1980s when people discussed the unique nature of humanity, they habitually used chess as primary proof of human superiority. They believed that computers would never beat humans at chess. On 10 February 1996, IBM's Deep Blue defeated world chess champion Garry Kasparov, laying to rest that particular claim for human pre-eminence.

Deep Blue was given a head start by its creators, who preprogrammed it not only with the basic rules of chess, but also with detailed instructions regarding chess strategies. A new generation of AI prefers machine learning to human advice. In February 2015 a program developed by Google DeepMind learned *by itself* how to play forty-nine classic Atari games, from *Pac-Man* to car racing. It then played most of them as well as or better than humans, sometimes coming up with strategies that never occur to human players.

Shortly afterwards AI scored an even more sensational success, when Google's AlphaGo software taught itself how to play Go, an ancient Chinese strategy board game significantly more complex than chess. Go's intricacies were long considered far beyond the reach of AI programs. In March 2016 a match was held in Seoul between AlphaGo and the South Korean Go champion, Lee Sedol. AlphaGo trounced Lee 4–1 by employing unorthodox moves and original strategies that stunned the experts. Whereas prior to the match most professional Go players were certain that Lee would win, after analysing

AlphaGo's moves most concluded that the game was up and that humans no longer had any hope of beating AlphaGo and its progeny.

Computer algorithms have recently proven their worth in ball games, too. For many decades, baseball teams used the wisdom, experience and gut instincts of professional scouts and managers to pick players. The best players fetched millions of dollars, and naturally enough the rich teams grabbed the cream of the crop, whereas poorer teams had to settle for the scraps. In 2002 Billy Beane, the manager of the low-budget Oakland Athletics, decided to beat the system. He relied on an arcane computer algorithm developed by economists and computer geeks to create a winning team from players whom human scouts had overlooked or undervalued. Old-timers were incensed that Beane's algorithm had violated the hallowed halls of baseball. They insisted that picking baseball players is an art, and that only humans with an intimate and long-standing experience of the game can master it. A computer program could never do it, because it could never decipher the secrets and the spirit of baseball.

They soon had to eat their baseball caps. Beane's shoestring-budget ($44 million) algorithmic team not only held its own against baseball giants such as the New York Yankees ($125 million), but became the first team in American League history ever to win twenty consecutive games. Not that Beane and Oakland got to enjoy their success for long. Soon enough many other teams adopted the same algorithmic approach, and since the Yankees and Red Sox could pay far more for both baseball players and computer software, low-budget teams such as the Oakland Athletics ended up having an even smaller chance of beating the system than before.

In 2004 Professor Frank Levy from MIT and Professor Richard Murnane from Harvard published a thorough research of the job market, listing those professions most likely to undergo automation. Truck driving was given as an example of a job that could not possibly be automated in the foreseeable future. It is hard to imagine, they wrote, that algorithms could safely drive trucks on a busy road. A mere ten years later Google and Tesla can not only imagine this, but are actually making it happen.

In fact, as time goes by it becomes easier and easier to replace humans with computer algorithms, not merely because the algorithms are getting smarter, but also because humans are professionalising. Ancient hunter-gatherers mastered a very wide variety of skills in order to survive, which is why it would be immensely difficult to design a robotic hunter-gatherer. Such a robot would have to know how to prepare stone tools, find edible mushrooms in a forest and track down prey.

However, over the last few thousand years we humans have been specialising. A taxi driver or a cardiologist specialises in a much narrower niche than a hunter-gatherer, which makes it easier to replace them with AI. As I have repeatedly stressed, AI is nowhere near human-like existence. But 99 per cent of human qualities and abilities are simply redundant for the performance of most modern jobs. For AI to squeeze humans out of the job market it needs only to outperform us in the specific abilities a particular profession demands.

Even the managers in charge of all these activities can be replaced. Thanks to its powerful algorithms, Uber can manage millions of taxi drivers with only a handful of humans. Most of the commands are given by the algorithms without any need of human supervision. In May 2014 Deep Knowledge Ventures – a Hong Kong venture-capital firm specialising in regenerative medicine – broke new ground by appointing an algorithm named VITAL to its board. Like the other five board members, VITAL gets to vote on whether or not the firm invests in a specific company, basing its opinions on a meticulous analysis of huge amounts of data.

Examining VITAL's record so far, it seems that it has already picked up at least one managerial vice: nepotism. It has recommended investing in companies that grant algorithms more authority. For example, with VITAL's blessing, Deep Knowledge Ventures has recently invested in Pathway Pharmaceuticals, which employs an algorithm called OncoFinder to select and rate personalised cancer therapies.

As algorithms push humans out of the job market, wealth and power might become concentrated in the hands of the tiny elite that owns the all-powerful algorithms, creating unprecedented social and political inequality. Today millions of taxi drivers, bus drivers and truck drivers have significant economic and political clout, each commanding a tiny share of the transportation market. If their collective interests are threatened, they can unionise, go on strike, stage boycotts and create powerful voting blocks. However, once millions of human drivers are replaced by a single algorithm, all that wealth and power will be cornered by the corporation that owns the algorithm, and by the handful of billionaires who own the corporation.

Alternatively, the algorithms might themselves become the owners. Human law already recognises intersubjective entities like corporations and nations as 'legal persons'. Though Toyota or Argentina has neither a body nor a mind, they are subject to international laws, they can own land and money, and they can sue and be sued in court. We might soon grant similar status to algorithms. An algorithm could then own a transportation empire or a venture-capital fund without having to obey the wishes of any human master.

If the algorithm makes the right decisions, it could accumulate a fortune, which it could then invest as it sees fit, perhaps buying your house and becoming your landlord. If you infringe on the algorithm's legal rights – say, by not paying rent – the algorithm could hire lawyers and sue you in court. If such algorithms consistently outperform human capitalists, we might end up with an algorithmic upper class owning most of our planet. This may sound impossible, but before dismissing the idea, remember that most of our planet is already legally owned by non-human intersubjective entities, namely nations and corporations. Indeed, 5,000 years ago much of Sumer was owned by imaginary gods such as Enki and Inanna. If gods can possess land and employ people, why not algorithms?

So what will people do? Art is often said to provide us with our ultimate (and uniquely human) sanctuary. In a world where computers have replaced doctors, drivers, teachers and even landlords, would everyone become an artist? Yet it is hard to see why artistic creation would be safe from the algorithms. Why are we so confident that computers will never be able to outdo us in the composition of music? According to the life sciences, art is not the product of some enchanted spirit or metaphysical soul, but rather of organic algorithms recognising mathematical patterns. If so, there is no reason why non-organic algorithms couldn't master it.

David Cope is a musicology professor at the University of California in Santa Cruz. He is also one of the more controversial figures in the world of classical music. Cope has written computer programs that compose concertos, chorales, symphonies and operas. His first creation was named EMI (Experiments in Musical Intelligence), which specialised in imitating the style of Johann Sebastian Bach. It took seven years to create the program, but once the work was done EMI composed 5,000 chorales à la Bach in a single day. Cope arranged for a performance of a few select chorales at a music festival in Santa Cruz. Enthusiastic members of the audience praised the stirring performance, and explained excitedly how the music had touched their innermost being. They didn't know that it had been created by EMI rather than Bach, and when the truth was revealed some reacted with glum silence, while others shouted in anger.

EMI continued to improve and learned to imitate Beethoven, Chopin, Rachmaninov and Stravinsky. Cope got EMI a contract and its first album – *Classical Music Composed by Computer* – sold surprisingly well. Publicity brought increasing hostility from classical-music buffs. Professor Steve Larson from the University of Oregon sent Cope a challenge for a musical showdown. Larson suggested that professional pianists play three pieces one after the other: one each by Bach, by EMI, and by Larson himself. The audience would then be asked to vote on who composed which piece. Larson was convinced that people would easily distinguish between soulful human compositions and the lifeless artefact of a machine. Cope accepted the challenge. On the appointed date hundreds of lecturers, students and music fans assembled in the University of Oregon's concert hall. At the end of the performance, a vote was taken. The result? The audience thought that EMI's piece was genuine Bach, that Bach's piece was composed by Larson, and that Larson's piece was produced by a computer.

Critics continued to argue that EMI's music is technically excellent, but that it lacks something. It is too accurate. It has no depth. It has no soul. Yet when people heard EMI's compositions without being informed of their provenance, they frequently praised them precisely for their soulfulness and emotional resonance.

Following EMI's successes Cope created newer and even more sophisticated programs. His crowning achievement was Annie. Whereas EMI composed music according to predetermined rules, Annie is based on machine learning. Its musical style constantly changes and develops in response to new input from the outside world. Cope has no idea what Annie is going to compose next. Indeed, Annie does not restrict itself to music composition, but also explores other art forms such as haiku poetry. In 2011 Cope published *Comes the Fiery Night: 2,000 Haiku by Man and Machine. Some* of the haiku were written by Annie and the rest by organic poets. The book does not disclose which are which. If you think you can tell the difference between human creativity and machine output, you are welcome to test your claim.

In the nineteenth century the Industrial Revolution created a huge new class of urban proletariats, and socialism spread because no other creed managed to answer the unprecedented needs, hopes and fears of this new working class. Liberalism eventually defeated socialism only by adopting the best parts of the socialist programme. In the twenty-first century we might witness the creation of a massive new unworking class: people devoid of any economic, political or even artistic value, who contribute nothing to the prosperity, power and glory of society. This 'useless class' will not be merely unemployed – it will be unemployable.

In September 2013 two Oxford researchers, Carl Benedikt Frey and Michael A. Osborne, published 'The Future of Employment', in which they surveyed the likelihood of different professions being taken over by computer algorithms within the next twenty years. The algorithm developed by Frey and Osborne to do the calculations estimated that 47 per cent of US jobs are at high risk. For example, there is a 99 per cent probability that by 2033 human telemarketers and insurance underwriters will lose their jobs to algorithms. There is a 98 per cent probability that the same will happen to sports referees, 97 per cent that it will happen to cashiers and 96 per cent to chefs. Waiters – 94 per cent. Paralegal assistants – 94 per cent. Tour guides – 91 per cent. Bakers – 89 per cent. Bus drivers – 89 per cent. Construction labourers – 88 per cent. Veterinary assistants – 86 per cent. Security guards – 84 per cent. Sailors – 83 per cent. Bartenders – 77 per cent. Archivists – 76 per cent. Carpenters – 72 per cent. Lifeguards – 67 per cent. And so forth. There are of course some safe jobs. The likelihood that computer algorithms will displace archaeologists by 2033 is only 0.7 per cent, because their job requires highly sophisticated types of pattern recognition, and doesn't produce huge profits. Hence it is improbable that corporations or government will make the necessary investment to automate archaeology within the next twenty years.

Of course, by 2033 many new professions are likely to appear, for example, virtual-world designers. But such professions will probably require much more creativity and flexibility than current run-of-the-mill jobs, and it is unclear whether forty-year-old cashiers or insurance agents will be able to reinvent themselves as virtual-world designers (try to imagine a virtual world created by an insurance agent!). And even if they do so, the pace of progress is such that within another decade they might have to reinvent themselves yet again. After all, algorithms might well outperform humans in designing virtual worlds too. The crucial problem isn't creating new jobs. The crucial problem is creating new jobs that humans perform better than algorithms.

Since we do not know what the job market will look like in 2030 or 2040, already today we have no idea what to teach our kids. Most of what they currently learn at school will probably be irrelevant by the time they are forty. Traditionally, life has been divided into two main parts: a period of learning followed by a period of working. Very soon this traditional model will become utterly obsolete, and the only way for humans to stay in the game will be to keep learning throughout their lives, and to reinvent themselves repeatedly. Many if not most humans may be unable to do so.

The coming technological bonanza will probably make it feasible to feed and support these useless masses even without any effort from their side. But what will keep them occupied and content? People must do something, or they go crazy. What will they do all day? One answer might be drugs and computer games. Unnecessary people might spend increasing amounts of time within 3D virtual-reality worlds, that would provide them with far more excitement and emotional engagement than the drab reality outside. Yet such a development would deal a mortal blow to the liberal belief in the sacredness of human life and of human experiences. What's so sacred about useless bums who pass their days devouring artificial experiences in La La Land?

Some experts and thinkers, such as Nick Bostrom, warn that humankind is unlikely to suffer this degradation, because once artificial intelligence surpasses human intelligence, it might simply exterminate humankind. The AI would likely do so either for fear that humankind would turn against it and try to pull its plug, or in pursuit of some unfathomable goal of its own. For it would be extremely difficult for humans to control the motivation of a system smarter than themselves.

Even preprogramming the system with seemingly benign goals might backfire horribly. One popular scenario imagines a corporation designing the first artificial super-intelligence and giving it an innocent test such as calculating pi. Before anyone realises what is happening, the AI takes over the planet, eliminates the human race, launches a campaign of conquest to the ends of the galaxy, and transforms the entire known universe into a giant super-computer that for billions upon billions of years calculates pi ever more accurately. After all, this is the divine mission its Creator gave it.

A Probability of 87 Per Cent

AT THE BEGINNING of this chapter we identified several practical threats to liberalism. The first is that humans might become militarily and economically useless. This is just a possibility, of course, not a prophecy. Technical difficulties or political objections might slow down the algorithmic invasion of the job market. Alternatively, since much of the human mind is still uncharted territory, we don't really know what hidden talents humans might discover in themselves, and what novel jobs they might create to offset the loss of others. That, however, may not be enough to save liberalism. For liberalism believes not just in the value of human beings – it also believes in individualism. The second threat facing liberalism is that while the system might still need humans in the future, it will not need individuals. Humans will continue to compose music, teach physics and invest money, but the system will understand these humans better than they understand themselves and will make most of the important decisions for them. The system will thereby deprive individuals of their authority and freedom.

The liberal belief in individualism is founded on the three important assumptions that we discussed earlier:

1. I am an in-dividual – that is, I have a single essence that cannot be divided into parts or subsystems. True, this inner core is wrapped in many outer layers. But if I make the effort to peel away these external crusts, I will find deep within myself a clear and single inner voice, which is my authentic self.
2. My authentic self is completely free.
3. It follows from the first two assumptions that I can know things about myself nobody else can discover. For only I have access to my inner space of freedom, and only I can hear the whispers of my authentic self. This is why liberalism grants the individual so much authority. I cannot trust anyone else to make choices for me, because no one else can know who I really am, how I feel and what I want. This is why the voter knows best, why the customer is always right and why beauty is in the eye of the beholder.

However, the life sciences challenge all three assumptions. According to them:

1. Organisms are algorithms, and humans are not individuals – they are 'dividuals'. That is, humans are an assemblage of many different algorithms lacking a single inner voice or a single self.
2. The algorithms constituting a human are not free. They are shaped by genes and environmental pressures, and take decisions either deterministically or randomly – but not freely.
3. It follows that an external algorithm could theoretically know me much better than I can ever know myself. An algorithm that monitors each of the systems that comprise my body and my brain could know exactly who I am, how I feel and what I want. Once developed, such an algorithm could replace the voter, the customer and the beholder. Then the algorithm will know best, the algorithm will always be right, and beauty will be in the calculations of the algorithm.

During the nineteenth and twentieth centuries the belief in individualism nevertheless made good practical sense, because there were no external algorithms that could actually monitor me effectively. States and markets may have wished to do exactly that, but they lacked the necessary technology. The KGB and FBI had only a vague understanding of my biochemistry, genome and brain, and even if agents bugged every phone call I made and recorded every chance encounter on the street, they did not have the computing power to analyse all that data. Consequently, given twentieth-century technological conditions, liberals were right to argue that nobody can know me better than I know myself. Humans therefore had a very good reason to regard themselves as an autonomous system and to follow their own inner voices rather than the commands of Big Brother.

However, twenty-first-century technology may enable external algorithms to 'hack humanity' and know me far better than I know myself. Once this happens the belief in individualism will collapse and authority will shift from individual humans to networked algorithms. People will no longer see themselves as autonomous beings running their lives according to their wishes, but instead will become accustomed to seeing themselves as a collection of biochemical mechanisms that is constantly monitored and guided by a network of electronic algorithms. For this to happen there is no need of an external algorithm that knows me *perfectly* and never makes a mistake; it is enough that the algorithm will know me *better* than I know myself and will make *fewer* mistakes than I do. It will then make sense to trust this algorithm with more and more of my decisions and life choices.

We have already crossed this line as far as medicine is concerned. In hospitals we are no longer individuals. It is highly likely that during your lifetime many of the most momentous decisions about your body and your health will be taken by computer algorithms such as IBM's

Watson. And this is not necessarily bad news. Diabetics already carry sensors that automatically check their sugar level several times a day, alerting them whenever it crosses a dangerous threshold. In 2014 researchers at Yale University announced the first successful trial of an 'artificial pancreas' controlled by an iPhone. Fifty-two diabetics took part in the experiment. Each patient had a tiny sensor and a tiny pump implanted in his or her abdomen. The pump was connected to small tubes of insulin and glucagon, two hormones that together regulate sugar levels in the blood. The sensor constantly measured the sugar level, transmitting the data to an iPhone. The iPhone hosted an application that analysed the information, and whenever necessary gave orders to the pump, which injected measured amounts of either insulin or glucagon – without any need of human intervention.

Many other people who suffer from no serious illnesses have begun to use wearable sensors and computers to monitor their health and activities. These devices – incorporated into anything from smartphones and wristwatches to armbands and underwear – record diverse biometric data such as blood pressure and heart rate. The data is then fed into sophisticated computer programs, that advise the wearer how to alter his or her diet and daily routines in order to enjoy improved health and a longer and more productive life. Google, together with the drug giant Novartis, is developing a contact lens that checks glucose levels in the blood every few seconds, by analysing the composition of tears. Pixie Scientific sells 'smart diapers' that analyse baby poop for clues about the child's medical condition. In November 2014 Microsoft launched the Microsoft Band – a smart armband that monitors among other things your heartbeat, the quality of your sleep and the number of steps you take each day. An application called Deadline goes a step further, informing you how many years of life you have left, given your current habits.

Some people use these apps without thinking too deeply about it, but for others this is already an ideology, if not a religion. The Quantified Self movement argues that the self is nothing but mathematical patterns. These patterns are so complex that the human mind has no chance of understanding them. So if you wish to obey the old adage and know thyself, you should not waste your time on philosophy, meditation or psychoanalysis, but rather you should systematically collect biometric data and allow algorithms to analyse them for you and tell you who you are and what you should do. The movement's motto is 'Self-knowledge through numbers'.

In 2000 the Israeli singer Shlomi Shavan conquered the local playlists with his hit song 'Arik'. It's about a guy who is obsessed with his girlfriend's ex, named Arik. He demands to know who is better in bed – he, or Arik? The girlfriend dodges the question, saying that it was different with each of them. The guy is not satisfied and demands: 'Talk numbers, lady.' Well, precisely for such guys a company called Bedpost sells biometric armbands that you can wear while having sex. The armband collects data such as heart rate, sweat level, duration of sexual inter-course, duration of orgasm and the number of calories you burned. The data is fed into a computer that analyses the information and ranks your performance with precise numbers. No more fake orgasms and 'How was it for you?'

People who experience themselves through the unre-lenting mediation of such devices may begin to see themselves more as a collection of biochemical systems than as individuals, and their decisions will increasingly reflect the conflicting demands of the various systems. Suppose you have two free hours a week, and are uncer-tain whether to use them playing chess or tennis. A good friend might ask: 'What does your heart tell you?' 'Well,' you answer, 'as far as my heart is concerned, it's obvious tennis is better. It's also better for my cholesterol level and blood pressure. But my fMRI scans indicate I should strengthen my left pre-frontal cortex. In my family dementia is quite common, and my uncle had it at a very early age. The latest studies indicate that a weekly game of chess can help delay its onset.'

You can already find much more extreme examples of external mediation in the geriatric wards of hospitals. Humanism fantasises about old age as a period of wisdom and awareness. The ideal elder may suffer from bodily ail-ments and weaknesses, but his mind is quick and sharp, and he has eighty years of insights to dispense. He knows exactly what's what, and always has astute advice for the grandchildren and other visitors. Twenty-first-century octogenarians don't always conform to that image. Thanks to our growing understanding of human biology, medicine can keep us alive long enough for our minds and 'authentic selves' to disintegrate and dissolve. All too often, what's left is a collection of dysfunctional biological systems kept going by a collection of monitors, computers and pumps.

At a deeper level, as genetic technologies are integrated into daily life and people develop increasingly intimate relations with their DNA, the single self might blur even further and the authentic inner voice might dissolve into a noisy crowd of genes. When faced by difficult dilemmas and decisions, I may stop searching for my inner voice and instead consult my inner genetic parliament.

On 14 May 2013 the actress Angelina Jolie published an article in the *New York Times* about her decision to have a double mastectomy. Jolie had lived for years under the shadow of breast cancer, as both her mother and grandmother died of it at a relatively early age. Jolie herself did a genetic test that confirmed she was carrying a dangerous mutation of the BRCA1 gene. According to recent statistical surveys, women carrying this mutation have an 87 per cent probability of developing breast cancer. Even though at the time Jolie did not have cancer, she decided to pre-empt the dreaded disease and have a double mastectomy. In the article Jolie explained that 'I choose not to keep my story private because there are many women who do not know that they might be living under the shadow of cancer. It is my hope that they, too, will be able to get gene-tested, and that if they have a high risk they, too, will know that they have strong options.'

Deciding whether or not to undergo a mastectomy is a difficult and potentially fatal choice. Beyond the discomforts, dangers and financial costs of the operation and its follow-up treatments, the decision can have far-reaching effects on one's health, body image, emotional well-being and relationships. Jolie's choice, and the courage she showed in going public with it, caused a great stir and won her international acclaim and admiration. In particular, many hoped that the publicity would increase awareness of genetic medicine and its potential benefits.

From a historical perspective, it is interesting to note the critical role algorithms played in her case. When Jolie had to take such an important decision about her life, she did not climb a mountaintop overlooking the ocean, watch the sun set into the waves and attempt to connect to her innermost feelings. Instead, she preferred to listen to her genes, whose voice manifested not in feelings but in numbers. At the time, Jolie felt no pain or discomfort whatsoever. Her feelings told her: 'Relax, everything is perfectly fine.' But the computer algorithms used by her doctors told a different story: 'You don't feel anything is wrong, but there is a time bomb ticking in your DNA. Do something about it – now!'

Of course, Jolie's emotions and unique personality played a key part too. If another woman with a different personality had discovered she was carrying the same genetic mutation, she might well have decided not to undergo a mastectomy. However – and here we enter the twilight zone – what if that other woman had discovered she was carrying not only the dangerous BRCA1 muta-tion, but another mutation in the (fictional) gene ABCD3, which impairs a brain area responsible for evaluating probabilities, thereby causing people to underestimate dangers? What if a statistician pointed out to this woman that her mother, grandmother and several other relatives all died young because they underestimated various health risks and failed to take precautionary measures?

In all likelihood you too will make important decisions about your health in the same way as Angelina Jolie. You will undergo a genetic test, a blood test or an fMRI; an algorithm will analyse the results on the basis of enor-mous statistical databases; and you will then accept the algorithm's recommendation. This is not an apocalyptic scenario. Algorithms won't revolt and enslave us. Rather, they will be so good at making decisions for us that it would be madness not to follow their advice.

ANGELINA JOLIE'S FIRST leading role was in the 1993 science-fiction action film *Cyborg 2*. She played Casella Reese, a cyborg developed in the year 2074 by Pinwheel Robotics for corporate espionage and assassination.

Casella is programmed with human emotions, in order to blend better into human societies while pursuing her missions. When Casella discovers that Pinwheel Robotics not only controls her, but also intends to terminate her, she escapes and fights for her life and freedom. *Cyborg 2* is a liberal fantasy about an individual fighting for liberty and privacy against global corporate octopuses.

In her real life Jolie preferred to sacrifice privacy and autonomy for health. A similar desire to improve human health may well cause most of us to willingly dismantle the barriers protecting our private spaces and allow state bureaucracies and multinational corporations access to our innermost recesses. For instance, allowing Google to read our emails and follow our activities would make it possible for Google to alert us to brewing epidemics before they are noticed by traditional health services.

How does the UK National Health Service know that a flu epidemic has erupted in London? By analysing the reports of thousands of doctors in hundreds of clinics. And how do all these doctors get the information? Well, when Mary wakes up one morning feeling a bit under the weather, she doesn't run straight to her doctor. She waits a few hours, or even a day or two, hoping that a nice cup of tea with honey will do the trick. When things don't improve, she makes an appointment with the doctor, goes to the clinic and describes her symptoms. The doctor types the data into a computer, and hopefully somebody up in NHS headquarters analyses these data, together with reports streaming in from thousands of other doctors, and concludes that flu is on the march. All this takes a lot of time.

Google could do it in minutes. It merely needs to monitor the words Londoners type in their emails and in Google's search engine and cross-reference them with a database of disease symptoms. Suppose on an average day the words 'headache', 'fever', 'nausea' and 'sneezing' appear 100,000 times in London emails and searches. If today the Google algorithm notices they appear 300,000 times, then bingo! We have a flu epidemic. There is no need to wait till Mary goes to her doctor. On the very first morning she woke up feeling a bit unwell and before going to work she emailed a colleague, 'I have a headache, but I'll be there.' That's all Google needs.

However, for Google to work its magic Mary must allow Google not only to read her messages, but also to share the information with the health authorities. If Angelina Jolie was willing to sacrifice her privacy in order to raise awareness of breast cancer, why shouldn't Mary make a similar sacrifice in order to thwart epidemics?

This isn't a theoretical idea. In 2008 Google actually launched Google Flu Trends, that tracks flu outbreaks by monitoring Google searches. The service is still being developed, and due to privacy limitations it tracks only search words and allegedly avoids reading private emails. But it is already capable of ringing the flu alarm bells ten days before traditional health services.

The Google Baseline Study is an even more ambitious project. Google intends to build a mammoth database on human health, establishing the 'perfect health' profile. Identifying even the smallest deviations from the baseline will hopefully make it possible to alert people to burgeoning health problems such as cancer when they can be nipped in the bud. The Baseline Study dovetails with an entire line of products called Google Fit, that will be incorporated into wearables such as clothes, bracelets, shoes and glasses, and will collect a never-ending stream of biometrical data. The idea is for Google Fit products to collect the never-ending stream of biometrical data to feed the Baseline Study.

Yet companies such as Google want to go much deeper than wearables. The market for DNA testing is currently growing in leaps and bounds. One of its leaders is 23andMe, a private company founded by Anne Wojcicki, former wife of Google co-founder Sergey Brin. The name '23andMe' refers to the twenty-three pairs of chromosomes that encode the human genome, the message being that my chromosomes have a very special relationship with me. Whoever can understand what the chromosomes are saying can tell you things about yourself that you never even suspected.

If you want to know what, pay 23andMe a mere $99, and they will send you a small package with a tube. You spit into the tube, seal it and mail it to Mountain View, California. There the DNA in your saliva is read, and you receive the results online. You get a list of the potential health hazards you face, and your genetic predisposition to more than ninety traits and conditions ranging from baldness to blindness. 'Know thyself' was never easier or cheaper. Since it is all based on statistics, the size of the company's database is the key to making accurate predictions. Hence the first company to build a giant genetic database will provide customers with the best predictions, and will potentially corner the market. US biotech companies are increasingly worried that strict privacy laws in the USA combined with Chinese disregard for individual privacy may hand China the genetic market on a plate.

If we connect all the dots, and if we give Google and its competitors free access to our biometric devices, to our DNA scans and to our medical records, we will get an all-knowing medical health service, that will not only fight epidemics, but will also shield us from cancer, heart attacks and Alzheimer's. Yet with such a database at its disposal Google could do far more. Imagine a system that, in the words of the famous Police song, watches every breath you take, every move you make and every bond you break; a system that monitors your bank account and your heartbeat, your sugar levels and your sexual escapades. It will definitely know you much better than you know yourself. The self-deceptions and self-delusions that trap people in bad relationships, wrong careers and harmful habits will not fool Google. Unlike the narrating self that controls us today, Google will not make decisions on the basis of cooked-up stories, and will not be misled by cognitive short cuts and the peak-end rule. Google will actually remember every step we took and every hand we shook.

Many of us would be happy to transfer much of our decision-making processes into the hands of such a system, or at least consult with it whenever we face important choices. Google will advise us which movie to see, where to go on holiday, what to study in college, which job offer to accept, and even whom to date and marry. 'Listen, Google,' I will say, 'both John and Paul are courting me. I like both of them, but in different ways, and it's so hard to make up my mind. Given everything you know, what do you advise me to do?'

And Google will answer: 'Well, I've known you from the day you were born. I have read all your emails, recorded all your phone calls, and know your favourite films, your DNA and the entire biometric history of your heart. I have exact data about each date you went on and, if you want, I can show you second-by-second graphs of your heart rate, blood pressure and sugar levels whenever you went on a date with John or Paul. If necessary, I can even provide you with an accurate mathematical ranking of every sexual encounter you had with either of them. And naturally, I know them as well as I know you. Based on all this information, on my superb algorithms, and on decades' worth of statistics about millions of relationships – I advise you to go with John, with an 87 per cent probability that you will be more satisfied with him in the long run.

'Indeed, I know you so well that I also know you don't like this answer. Paul is much more handsome than John, and because you give external appearances too much weight, you secretly wanted me to say "Paul". Looks matter, of course; but not as much as you think. Your biochemical algorithms – which evolved tens of thousands of years ago on the African savannah – give looks a weight of 35 per cent in their overall rating of potential mates. My algorithms – which are based on the most up-to-date studies and statistics – say that looks have only a 14 per cent impact on the long-term success of romantic relationships. So, even though I took Paul's looks into account, I still tell you that you would be better off with John.'

In exchange for such devoted counselling services, we will just have to give up the idea that humans are individuals, and that each human has a free will determining what's good, what's beautiful and what is the meaning of life. Humans will no longer be autonomous entities directed by the stories their narrating self invents. Instead, they will be integral parts of a huge global network.

LIBERALISM SANCTIFIES THE narrating self, and allows it to vote in the polling stations, in the supermarket and in the marriage market. For centuries this made good sense, because though the narrating self believed in all kinds of fictions and fantasies, no alternative system knew me better. Yet once we have a system that really does know me better, it will be foolhardy to leave authority in the hands of the narrating self.

Liberal habits such as democratic elections will become obsolete, because Google will be able to represent even my own political opinions better than I can. When I stand behind the curtain in the polling booth, liberalism instructs me to consult my authentic self and choose whichever party or candidate reflects my deepest desires. Yet the life sciences point out that when I stand there behind that curtain, I don't really remember everything I felt and thought in the years since the last election. Moreover, I am bombarded by a barrage of propaganda, spin and random memories that might well distort my choices. Just as in Kahneman's cold-water experiment, in politics too the narrating self follows the peak-end rule. It forgets the vast majority of events, remembers only a few extreme incidents and gives a wholly disproportionate weight to recent happenings.

For four long years I may have repeatedly complained about the PM's policies, telling myself and anyone willing to listen that he will be 'the ruin of us all'. However, in the months prior to the election the government cuts taxes and spends money generously. The ruling party hires the best copywriters to lead a brilliant campaign, with a well-balanced mixture of threats and promises that speak directly to the fear centre in my brain. On the morning of the election I wake up with a cold, which impacts my mental processes and induces me to prefer security and stability over all other considerations. And voila! I send the man who will be 'the ruin of us all' back into office for another four years.

I could have saved myself from such a fate if only I had authorised Google to vote for me. Google wasn't born yesterday, you know. Though it won't ignore the recent tax cuts and the election promises, it will also remember what happened throughout the previous four years. It will know what my blood pressure was every time I read the morning newspapers, and how my dopamine level plummeted while I watched the evening news. Google will know how to screen the spin-doctors' empty slogans. Google will understand that illness makes voters lean a bit more to the right than usual, and will compensate for this. Google will therefore be able to vote not according to my momentary state of mind, and not according to the fantasies of the narrating self, but rather according to the real feelings and interests of the collection of biochemical algorithms known as 'I'.

Naturally, Google will not always get it right. After all, these are all just probabilities. But if Google makes enough good decisions, people will grant it increasing authority. As time goes by, the databases will grow, the statistics will become more accurate, the algorithms will improve and the decisions will be even better. The system will never know me perfectly, and will never be infallible. But there is no need for that. Liberalism will collapse on the day the system knows me better than I know myself. Which is less difficult than it may sound, given that most people don't really know themselves well.

A recent study commissioned by Google's nemesis – Facebook – has indicated that already today the Facebook algorithm is a better judge of human personalities and dispositions than even people's friends, parents and spouses. The study was conducted on 86,220 volunteers who have a Facebook account and who completed a hundred-item personality questionnaire. The Facebook algorithm predicted the volunteers' answers based on monitoring their Facebook Likes – which webpages, images and clips they tagged with the Like button. The more Likes, the more accurate the predictions. The algorithm's predictions were compared with those of work colleagues, friends, family members and spouses. Amazingly, the algorithm needed a set of only ten Likes in order to outperform the predictions of work colleagues. It needed seventy Likes to outperform friends, 150 Likes to outperform family members and 300 Likes to outperform spouses. In other words, if you happen to have clicked 300 Likes on your Facebook account, the Facebook algorithm can predict your opinions and desires better than your husband or wife!

Indeed, in some fields the Facebook algorithm did

better than the person themself. Participants were asked to evaluate things such as their level of substance use or the size of their social networks. Their judgements were less accurate than those of the algorithm. The research concludes with the following prediction (made by the human authors of the article, not by the Facebook algorithm): 'People might abandon their own psychological judgements and rely on computers when making important life decisions, such as choosing activities, career paths, or even romantic partners. It is possible that such data-driven decisions will improve people's lives.'

On a more sinister note, the same study implies that in future US presidential elections Facebook could know not only the political opinions of tens of millions of Americans, but also who among them are the critical swing voters, and how these voters might be swung. Facebook could tell that in Oklahoma the race between Republicans and Democrats is particularly close, identify the 32,417 voters who still haven't made up their minds, and determine what each candidate needs to say in order to tip the balance. How could Facebook obtain this priceless political data? We provide it for free.

In the heyday of European imperialism, conquistadors and merchants bought entire islands and countries in exchange for coloured beads. In the twenty-first century our personal data is probably the most valuable resource most humans still have to offer, and we are giving it to the tech giants in exchange for email services and funny cat videos.

From Oracle to Sovereign

ONCE GOOGLE, FACEBOOK and other algorithms become all-knowing oracles, they may well evolve into agents and ultimately into sovereigns. To understand this trajectory, consider the case of Waze – a GPS-based navigational application that many drivers use nowadays. Waze isn't just a map. Its millions of users constantly update it about traffic jams, car accidents and police cars. Hence Waze knows to divert you away from heavy traffic, and bring you to your destination through the quickest possible route. When you reach a junction and your gut instinct tells you to turn right, but Waze instructs you to turn left, users sooner or later learn that they had better listen to Waze rather than to their feelings.

At first sight it seems that the Waze algorithm serves only as an oracle. You ask a question, the oracle replies, but it is up to you to make a decision. If the oracle wins your trust, however, the next logical step is to turn it into an agent. You give the algorithm only a final aim, and it acts to realise that aim without your supervision. In the case of Waze, this may happen when you connect Waze to a self-driving car, and tell Waze 'take the fastest route home' or 'take the most scenic route' or 'take the route which will result in the minimum amount of pollution'. You call the shots, but leave it to Waze to execute your commands.

Finally, Waze might become sovereign. Having so much power in its hands, and knowing far more than you, it may start manipulating you and the other drivers, shaping your desires and making your decisions for you. For example, suppose because Waze is so good, everybody starts using it. And suppose there is a traffic jam on route no. 1, while the alternative route no. 2 is relatively open. If Waze simply lets everybody know that, then all drivers will rush to route no. 2, and it too will be clogged. When everybody uses the same oracle, and everybody believes the oracle, the oracle turns into a sovereign. So Waze must think for us. Maybe it will inform only half the drivers that route no. 2 is open, while keeping this information secret from the other half. Thereby pressure will ease on route no. 1 without blocking route no. 2.

Microsoft is developing a far more sophisticated system called Cortana, named after an AI character in its popular *Halo* video-game series. Cortana is an AI personal assistant that Microsoft hopes to include as an integral feature of future versions of Windows. Users will be encouraged to allow Cortana access to all their files, emails and applications, so that it will get to know them and can thereby offer advice on myriad matters, as well as becoming a virtual agent representing the user's interests. Cortana could remind you to buy something for your wife's birthday, select the present, reserve a table at a restaurant and prompt you to take your medicine an hour before dinner. It could alert you that if you don't stop reading now, you will be late for an important business meeting. As you are about to enter the meeting, Cortana will warn that your blood pressure is too high and your dopamine level too low, and based on past statistics, you tend to make serious business mistakes in such circumstances. So you had better keep things tentative and avoid committing yourself or signing any deals.

Once Cortanas evolve from oracles to agents, they might start speaking directly with one another on their masters' behalf. It can begin innocently enough, with my Cortana contacting your Cortana to agree on a place and time for a meeting. Next thing I know, a potential employer will tell me not to bother sending a CV, but simply allow his Cortana to grill my Cortana. Or my Cortana may be approached by the Cortana of a potential lover, and the two will compare notes to decide whether it's a good match – completely unbeknown to their human owners.

As Cortanas gain authority, they may begin manipulating each other to further the interests of their masters, so that success in the job market or the marriage market may increasingly depend on the quality of your Cortana. Rich people owning the most up-to-date Cortana will have a decisive advantage over poor people with their older versions.

But the murkiest issue of all concerns the identity of Cortana's master. As we have seen, humans are not individuals, and they don't have a single unified self. Whose interests, then, should Cortana serve? Suppose my narrating self makes a New Year resolution to start a diet and go to the gym every day. A week later, when it is time for the gym, the experiencing self instructs Cortana to turn on the TV and order pizza. What should Cortana do? Should it obey the experiencing self, or the resolution taken a week earlier by the narrating self?

You may well wonder whether Cortana is really different from an alarm clock, which the narrating self sets in the evening, in order to wake the experiencing self in time for work. But Cortana will have far more power over me than an alarm clock. The experiencing self can silence the alarm clock by pressing a button. In contrast, Cortana will know me so well that it will know exactly what inner buttons to push in order to make me follow its 'advice'.

Microsoft's Cortana is not alone in this game. Google Now and Apple's Siri are headed in the same direction. Amazon too employs algorithms that constantly study you and then use their accumulated knowledge to recommend products. When I go to a physical bookstore I wander among the shelves and trust my feelings to choose the right book. When I visit Amazon's virtual shop, an algorithm immediately pops up and tells me: 'I know which books you liked in the past. People with similar tastes also tend to love this or that new book.'

And this is just the beginning. Today in the US more people read digital books than printed ones. Devices such as Amazon's Kindle are able to collect data on their users while they are reading. Your Kindle can, for example, monitor which parts of a book you read quickly, and which slowly; on which page you took a break, and on which sentence you abandoned the book, never to pick it up again. (Better tell the author to rewrite that bit.) If Kindle is upgraded with face recognition and biometric sensors, it will know how each sentence you read influenced your heart rate and blood pressure. It will know what made you laugh, what made you sad and what made you angry. Soon, books will read you while you are reading them. And whereas you quickly forget most of what you read, Amazon will never forget a thing. Such data will enable Amazon to choose books for you with uncanny precision. It will also enable Amazon to know exactly who you are, and how to turn you on and off.

Eventually we may reach a point when it will be impossible to disconnect from this all-knowing network even for a moment. Disconnection will mean death. If medical hopes are realised, future humans will incorporate into their bodies a host of biometric devices, bionic organs and nano-robots, which will monitor our health and defend us from infections, illnesses and damage. Yet these devices will have to be online 24/7, both in order to be updated with the latest medical developments, and to protect them from the new plagues of cyberspace. Just as my home computer is constantly attacked by viruses, worms and Trojan horses, so will be my pacemaker, hearing aid and nanotech immune system. If I don't update my body's anti-virus program regularly, I will wake up one day to discover that the millions of nano-robots coursing through my veins are now controlled by a North Korean hacker.

The new technologies of the twenty-first century may thus reverse the humanist revolution, stripping humans of their authority, and empowering non-human algorithms instead. If you are horrified by this direction, don't blame the computer geeks. The responsibility actually lies with the biologists. It is crucial to realise that this entire trend is fuelled more by biological insights than by computer science. It is the life sciences that concluded that organisms are algorithms. If this is not the case – if organisms function in an inherently different way to algorithms – then computers may work wonders in other fields, but they will not be able to understand us and direct our life, and they will certainly be incapable of merging with us. Yet once biologists concluded that organisms are algorithms, they dismantled the wall between the organic and inorganic, turned the computer revolution from a purely mechanical affair into a biological cataclysm, and shifted authority from individual humans to networked algorithms.

Some people are indeed horrified by this development, but the fact is that millions willingly embrace it. Already today many of us give up our privacy and our individuality by conducting much of our lives online, recording our every action, and becoming hysterical if connection to the net is

interrupted even for a few minutes. The shifting of authority from humans to algorithms is happening all around us,
not as a result of some momentous governmental decision,
but due to a flood of mundane personal choices.

If we are not careful the result might be an Orwellian
police state that constantly monitors and controls not
only all our actions, but even what happens inside our
bodies and our brains. Just think what uses Stalin could
have found for omnipresent biometric sensors – and what
uses Putin might yet find for them. However, while
defenders of human individuality fear a repetition of
twentieth-century nightmares and brace themselves to
resist familiar Orwellian foes, human individuality is now
facing an even bigger threat from the opposite direction.
In the twenty-first century the individual is more likely to
disintegrate gently from within than to be brutally
crushed from without.

Today most corporations and governments pay homage
to my individuality and promise to provide medicine, education and entertainment customised to my unique needs
and wishes. But in order to do so, corporations and governments first need to deconstruct me into biochemical
subsystems, monitor these subsystems with ubiquitous
sensors and decipher their working with powerful algorithms. In the process, the individual will transpire to be
nothing but a religious fantasy. Reality will be a mesh of
biochemical and electronic algorithms, without clear borders, and without individual hubs.

Upgrading Inequality

SO FAR WE have looked at two of the three practical threats to liberalism: firstly, that humans will lose their value completely; secondly, that humans will still be valuable collectively, but will lose their individual authority, and instead be managed by external algorithms. The system will still need you to compose symphonies, teach history or write computer code, but it will know you better than you know yourself, and will therefore make most of the important decisions for you – and you will be perfectly happy with that. It won't necessarily be a bad world; it will, however, be a post-liberal world.

The third threat to liberalism is that some people will remain both indispensable and undecipherable, but they will constitute a small and privileged elite of upgraded humans. These superhumans will enjoy unheard-of abilities and unprecedented creativity, which will allow them to go on making many of the most important decisions in the world. They will perform crucial services for the system, while the system could neither understand nor manage them. However, most humans will not be upgraded, and will consequently become an inferior caste dominated by both computer algorithms and the new superhumans.

Splitting humankind into biological castes will destroy the foundations of liberal ideology. Liberalism can coexist with socio-economic gaps. Indeed, since it favours liberty over equality, it takes such gaps for granted. However, liberalism still presupposes that all human beings have equal value and authority. From a liberal perspective, it is perfectly all right that one person is a billionaire living in a sumptuous chateau, whereas another is a poor peasant living in a straw hut. For according to liberalism, the peasant's unique experiences are still just as valuable as the billionaire's. That's why liberal authors write long novels about the experiences of poor peasants – and why even billionaires avidly read such books. If you go to see *Les Misérables* on Broadway or at Covent Garden, you will find that good seats can cost hundreds of dollars, and the audience's combined wealth probably runs into the billions, yet they still sympathise with Jean Valjean who served nineteen years in jail for stealing a loaf of bread to feed his starving nephews.

The same logic operates on election day, when the vote of the poor peasant counts for exactly the same as the billionaire's. The liberal solution for social inequality is to give equal value to different human experiences, instead of trying to create the same experiences for everyone. However, will this solution still work once rich and poor are separated not merely by wealth, but also by real biological gaps?

In her *New York Times* article, Angelina Jolie referred to the high costs of genetic testing. The test Jolie had taken costs $3,000 (not including the price of the actual mastectomy, the reconstructive surgery and related treatments). This in a world where 1 billion people earn less than $1 per day, and another 1.5 billion earn between $1 and $2 a day. Even if they work hard their entire life, these people will never be able to afford a $3,000 genetic test. And the economic gaps are at present only increasing. As of early 2016, the sixty-two richest people in the world were worth as much as the poorest 3.6 billion people! Since the world's population is about 7.2 billion, it means that these sixty-two billionaires together hold as much wealth as the entire bottom half of humankind.

The cost of DNA testing is likely to go down with time, but expensive new procedures are constantly being pioneered. So while old treatments will gradually come within reach of the masses, the elites will always remain a couple of steps ahead. Throughout history the rich have enjoyed many social and political advantages, but no huge biological gap ever separated them from the poor. Medieval aristocrats claimed that superior blue blood was flowing through their veins, and Hindu Brahmins insisted that they were naturally smarter than everyone else, but this was pure fiction. In the future, however, we may see real gaps in physical and cognitive abilities opening between an upgraded upper class and the rest of society.

When scientists are confronted with this scenario, their standard reply is that in the twentieth century too many medical breakthroughs began with the rich, but eventually benefited the entire population and helped to narrow rather than widen the social gaps. For example, vaccines and antibiotics at first profited mainly the upper classes in Western countries, but today they improve the lives of all humans everywhere.

However, the expectation that this process will be repeated in the twenty-first century may be just wishful thinking, for two important reasons. First, medicine is undergoing a tremendous conceptual revolution. Twentieth-century medicine aimed to heal the sick. Twenty-first-century medicine is increasingly aiming to upgrade the healthy. Healing the sick was an egalitarian project, because it assumed that there is a normative standard of physical and mental health that everyone can and should enjoy. If someone fell below the norm, it was the job of doctors to fix the problem and help him or her 'be like everyone'. In contrast, upgrading the healthy is an elitist project, because it rejects the idea of a universal standard applicable to all and seeks to give some individuals an edge over others. People want superior memories, above-average intelligence and first-class sexual abilities. If some form of upgrade becomes so cheap and common that everyone enjoys it, it will simply be considered the new baseline, which the next generation of treatments will strive to surpass.

Consequently by 2070 the poor could very well enjoy much better healthcare than today, but the gap separating them from the rich will nevertheless be much greater. People usually compare themselves to their more fortunate contemporaries rather than to their ill-fated ancestors. If you tell a poor American in a Detroit slum that he has access to much better healthcare than his great-grandparents did a century ago, it is unlikely to cheer him up. Indeed, such talk will sound terribly smug and condescending. 'Why should I compare myself to nineteenth-century factory workers or peasants?' he would retort. 'I want to live like the rich people on television, or at least like the folks in the affluent suburbs.' Similarly, if in 2070 you tell the lower classes that they enjoy better healthcare than in 2017, it might be very cold comfort to them, because they would be comparing themselves to the upgraded superhumans who dominate the world.

Moreover, despite all the medical breakthroughs we cannot be absolutely certain that in 2070 the poor will indeed enjoy better healthcare than today, because the state and the elite may lose interest in providing the poor with healthcare. In the twentieth century medicine benefited the masses because the twentieth century was the age of the masses. Twentieth-century armies needed millions of healthy soldiers, and economies needed millions of healthy workers. Consequently states established public health services to ensure the health and vigour of everyone. Our greatest medical achievements were the provision of mass-hygiene facilities, the campaigns of mass vaccinations and the eradication of mass epidemics. In 1914 the Japanese elite had a vested interest in vaccinating the poor and building hospitals and sewage systems in the slums, because if they wanted Japan to be a strong nation with a powerful army and a robust economy, they needed many millions of healthy soldiers and workers.

But the age of the masses may be over, and with it the age of mass medicine. As human soldiers and workers give way to algorithms, at least some elites may conclude that there is no point in providing improved or even standard levels of health for masses of useless poor people, and it is far more sensible to focus on upgrading a handful of superhumans beyond the norm.

Already today the birth rate is falling in technologically advanced countries such as Japan and South Korea, where prodigious efforts are invested in the upbringing and education of fewer and fewer children – from whom more and more is expected. How can huge developing countries like India, Brazil or Nigeria hope to compete with Japan? These countries resemble a long train. The elites in the first-class carriages enjoy health care, education and income levels on a par with the most developed nations in the world. However, the hundreds of millions of ordinary citizens who crowd the third-class carriages still suffer from widespread disease, ignorance and poverty. What would the Indian, Brazilian or Nigerian elites prefer to do in the coming century? Invest in fixing the problems of hundreds of millions of poor, or in upgrading a few million rich? Unlike in the twentieth century, when the elite had a stake in fixing the problems of the poor because they were militarily and economically vital, in the twenty-first century the most efficient (albeit ruthless) strategy might be to let go of the useless third-class carriages, and dash forward with the first class only. In order to compete with Japan, Brazil might need a handful of upgraded superhumans far more than millions of healthy ordinary workers.

How will liberal beliefs survive the appearance of superhumans with exceptional physical, emotional and intellectual abilities? What will happen if it turns out that such superhumans have fundamentally different experiences from normal Sapiens? What if superhumans are bored by novels about the experiences of lowly Sapiens thieves, whereas run-of-the-mill humans find soap operas about superhuman love affairs unintelligible?

The great human projects of the twentieth century – overcoming famine, plague and war – aimed to safeguard a universal norm of abundance, health and peace for everyone without exception. The new projects of the twenty-first century – gaining immortality, bliss and divinity – also hope to serve the whole of humankind. However, because these projects aim at surpassing rather than safeguarding the norm, they may well result in the creation of a new superhuman caste that will abandon its liberal roots and treat normal humans no better than nineteenth-century Europeans treated Africans.

If scientific discoveries and technological developments split humankind into a mass of useless humans and a small elite of upgraded superhumans, or if authority shifts altogether away from human beings into the hands of highly intelligent algorithms, then liberalism will collapse. What new religions or ideologies might fill the resulting vacuum and guide the subsequent evolution of our godlike descendants?

For more from Yuval Noah Harari (including notes to the extracts you've just read) see *Sapiens* and *Homo Deus*

YUVAL NOAH HARARI was born in Israel in 1976 and grew up in a secular Jewish family. He came to the UK in his twenties where he studied at Oxford before returning to Israel where he is currently a lecturer at the Hebrew University of Jerusalem, specialising in the Middle Ages and World History.

From a young age he was preoccupied by the big questions in life: is there justice in history, does power ensure happiness, and what – if anything – makes humans different from other animals? Writing *Sapiens: A Brief History of Humankind* was an attempt to answer these questions and the book has since become an international phenomenon attracting a legion of fans from Bill Gates and Barack Obama to Chris Evans and Jarvis Cocker. His follow-up, *Homo Deus: A Brief History of Tomorrow* sees him tackle questions about the future of humanity and has been a similar international sensation.

He is a vegan and meditates for two hours every day as well as attending extended Vipassana meditation retreats every year. He lives with his husband in Karmei Yosef, just outside Jerusalem.

RECOMMENDED BOOKS BY YUVAL NOAH HARARI:

Sapiens
Homo Deus

What do we spend our Money on?

Home
SALMAN RUSHDIE

VINTAGE MINIS

Babies
ANNE ENRIGHT

VINTAGE MINIS

Eating
NIGELLA LAWSON

VINTAGE MINIS

Drinking
JOHN CHEEVER

VINTAGE MINIS

VINTAGE MINIS

The Vintage Minis bring you some of the world's greatest writers on the experiences that make us human. These stylish, entertaining little books explore the whole spectrum of life – from birth to death, and everything in between. Which means there's something here for everyone, whatever your story.

vintageminis.co.uk